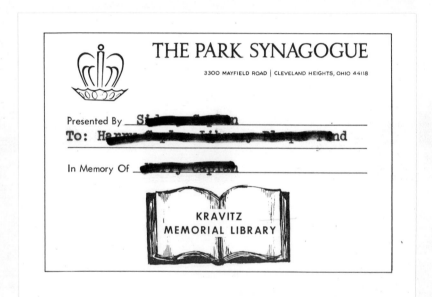

THE PARK SYNAGOGUE

3300 MAYFIELD ROAD | CLEVELAND HEIGHTS, OHIO 44118

Presented By ▬▬▬▬▬▬▬▬▬▬▬▬▬▬▬▬▬▬▬▬▬

To: ▬▬▬▬▬▬▬▬▬▬▬▬▬▬▬▬▬▬▬▬▬▬▬ nd

In Memory Of ▬▬▬▬▬▬▬▬▬▬▬▬▬▬▬▬▬▬▬

KRAVITZ
MEMORIAL LIBRARY

I Chose Life

I Chose Life

by
Samuel Gruber
as told to
Gertrude Hirschler

Introduction by
Howard L. Adelson

Shengold Publishers, Inc.
New York City

ISBN 0-88400-055-9
Library of Congress Catalog Card Number: 78-52141
Copyright © 1978 by Samuel Gruber
All rights reserved

Published by Shengold Publishers, Inc.
New York, N.Y.

Printed in the United States of America

*To my dear wife
and our children*

PREFACE

It is now more than three decades since the end of the Nazi Holocaust. Yet, writing this book has brought back such vivid memories that I felt as if all the events retold here happened only yesterday.

My son, Jack, has heard my story of the war years so many times he felt almost as if he had lived through them. "My father has a great deal to tell. Unbelievable things happened during the war, and we must know about them," maintains Jack. "The importance of this book is that it shows exactly what happened and how, even against overwhelming odds, some people were fortunate enough to resist the fate in store for them."

As my son was growing up, he often asked me to write a book but somehow I never got around to it. I felt that either it was too soon after the war or that the time was not right. Finally, about eight years ago, during our daily rides to New York City, I began to tape record my story.

I am glad that I was able to relate what I and my fellow-fighters underwent — first in the ghettos, then in the camps, and finally in the forests. Too many comrades, friends and fighters perished in the struggle, and in telling this story I believe I am fulfilling their dying wish that their sufferings should not be forgotten.

S.G.

ACKNOWLEDGMENTS

I should like to express my special thanks to Professor Howard L. Adelson for his most illuminating Introduction. Professor Adelson not only is a prominent historian but an astute commentator on current Jewish events, and has a specialized interest in the survivors of the Holocaust.

I am most grateful also to Mr. Maurice Bradley for recording my memories and to Miss Gertrude Hirschler for writing and editing the material. My thanks, too, to Dr. Freema Gottlieb, who put the finishing touches to the manuscript, and to Vicky Marlow for typing it.

My deep appreciation to my son, Jack, without whose constant urging this book would never have been written, and to my younger son, Mark, for reading the galley proofs.

And finally, it goes without saying that without the support, advice, and patience of my dear wife, it would have been impossible for me to see the completion of this book.

INTRODUCTION
by
Howard L. Adelson
Professor of History
City University of New York

In the modern world we have become so accustomed to the casual use of titles and superlatives that we lose sight of what real merit means. In one sense it is unfortunate that our generation has been called upon to a greater degree than others to demonstrate heroism of an unparalleled type. Ninety generations of Jewry have experienced anti-Semitism and hatred which beggars comparison with other forms of prejudice, but all of them pale before the tragedy of European Jewry in the Second World War. Even in the annals of Jewry, the suffering of the Polish Jews remains unique.

No self-respecting human being on this entire planet can today claim ignorance of how European Jewry was humiliated and tortured, confined in ghettoes with walls and guards, bereft of sympathy even from those who joined in opposing the Nazis, and finally consigned to torture and death by disease, maltreatment, starvation, and outright murder. That portion of the story of the martyrdom of modern Jewry has been told and retold, studied and analyzed. It is a gruesome tale which recounts the destruction of three out of every four Jews in Europe with a savagery that seems inconceivable to normal human beings in the Western world. The account of the incomparable fear that paralyzed masses of men and women can never be described in words. Those of us who never experienced the tragedy can only feel awe in the presence of its survivors. To fight against the murderers, however, was an act of bravery which surpasses even that of the Maccabees.

The circumstances under which the remnants of East European Jewry survived were especially difficult because the local population was also anti-Semitic. Even those who were supposedly engaged in the fight against the alien German conquerors paused in that struggle long enough to kill Jews or to inform against them to the Nazis. It was not by chance that the inhuman Nazi murderers chose Poland as the charnel house for European Jewry. With forethought they recognized that within Poland the neighbors of the Jews would assist in the slaughter. Flight was impossible because only very rarely was a Gentile prepared to save a Jew Even the Polish Home Army, the *Armja Krajova,* which was supposedly struggling against the Nazis, pursued the slaughter of the Jews with greater vigor than the war against the German conquerors. The local peasantry displayed an atavistic savagery that is unequalled in the annals of human history. Jews died while their neighbors exulted in their suffering. Prince Radziwill tells of how the Polish officers in captivity celebrated a record slaughter of the Jews in the extermination camps even though it meant defeat for Poland. Jews themselves lost faith in the future, and we know of an individual who wrote an entire Jewish prayer book (*siddur*) from memory by hand in the death camps because he felt certain that only thus could a trace of Jewry survive.

In the midst of this horror, a few brave men determined to survive, and also to fight back and to save other tortured Jews. The story of Jewish resistance is the best kept secret of the Second World War. To succeed in escaping from the Nazis, to survive in the hostile environment of the forest or the marsh with its roving bands of the *Armja Krajova* bent on killing Jews, and to secure weapons with which to fight as well as food and clothing required luck as well as courage. The odds against success were astronomical, as were also the odds against living through to liberation. Every individual who took part in the struggle had to admit to himself that his death was imminent. It should not be a matter of surprise to any of us that only the smallest handful were successful. Most perished in the early stages of their attempt to fight back. Nevertheless, particularly in central and eastern Europe, the Jews formed a very significant segment of the resistance movements. Despite the difficulties and the virtually universal anti-Semitism they fought back and hit the Nazis hard.

Even when an individual Jew managed to reach the forest, and to join one of the bands of resistance fighters, he found that anti-Semitism was his constant companion. The Jewish resistance groups were forced to coordinate their activities with those of the better armed and stronger non-Jewish groups. Often they were required to accept as commanders men who displayed their anti-Semitism openly, while on other occasions it was the policy of the Soviet Union to force Jewish units to merge with other groups and to lose their distinct Jewish identity. That was at best a dangerous position for the Jewish resistance fighters. As individuals survival was virtually impossible for them, and yet they knew that they could place no trust in the non-Jewish partisans many of whom were violently anti-Semitic. Life for the Jewish resistance fighters or partisans hung by a slender thread which could be brutally severed at any moment. Men and women lived from day to day and displayed unequalled heroism and loyalty to one another and to the Jewish people.

Partisans have always depended upon a friendly native population to supply them with food and clothing without which they could not survive. For the Jewish partisans this created unheard-of difficulties. The peasantry of eastern Europe had been infected by centuries of anti-Semitism, and the fact that the Germans placed a price on the head of any Jew trying to survive only served to stimulate the avarice of the non-Jew. Jewish partisans had to take unprecedented measures to instill fear into the peasantry lest they openly join the Germans in searching out and killing Jews. Great skill was required to obtain food and supplies. The non-Jewish resistance groups were often allied with peasant villages and heeded their complaints against Jewish "robbers and brigands." Jewish partisans had to prove their value in the fight against the German conquerors, if they were to be permitted to have food rations. Thus the most dangerous missions were assigned to them. Despite the risks inherent in their mission, the Jewish partisans attempted to carry it out and suffered the losses that came from challenging regular troops of the German army at its strongest.

Under these circumstances there was no time for record-keeping and war diaries such as are common in regular armies or even well organized guerrilla forces. Each little unit fought a very private war with minimal support and direction. They depended upon the initiative of the individual Jews who assumed command. A gentle people who had sought for hundreds of years to live in peace with their neighbors was transformed in the combat into a new race of Maccabees. The watchword with which they greeted one another, *"amcha"* ("Your (i.e. God's) people"),reflected the pride and unity which these brave men and women found in the gloomy forests and marshes of eastern Europe. To fight was to live for another day; to rest was to risk instant death. To fight was to preserve the honor and dignity of the Jewish people at its saddest moment; to accept fate was to accept ignominy.

How can the epic history of such deeds be told? Much that happened was lost when those who fought for survival died on the battlefield. A great deal more went unseen by those who might have preserved it. Without written records and with barely a handful of survivors alive only a pale reflection of the valiant Jewish partisans can be reconstructed from the memoirs of the victorious remnant. Each such account is a precious document in its own right; one that comes from the hand of a commander of a Jewish partisan unit is even more valuable. Samuel (Mietek) Gruber is a perfect example of such a Jewish partisan commander. Mobilized as a Polish soldier, he was wounded in combat with the Germans and then endured the unique hell reserved for the Jews in Nazi Europe. His tale, told in the stark language of a man of action, reveals that thirty years later those events and that suffering still live on. The romance of youth and the horror of death go hand in hand throughout the narrative, but the stark reality of the constant struggle for survival has never been erased. Mietek Gruber lived in a different world with savage rules for survival, and yet the intensely human emotions that motivated him are visible in this narrative. Those of us who did not experience that world can never fully hope to understand it, but we can stand in awe of what we do know to be the truth. It was a world in which danger was a constant companion and in which death was a common occurrence. Mietek Gruber, as his narrative shows, was a commander of heroes who postured and joked in the face of the enemy and yet never expected to witness the liberation. When it actually came, freedom was anti-climactic, and its aftermath far from consoling. As the battle-weary partisans lay concealed in a field of grain, the massed, armored might of the German army rolled by a short distance away in the retreat which ended the Nazi menace. Suddenly the partisans found themselves in supposedly friendly territory;

they should have been able to breathe freely once more. In fact such was not the case, and Jews continued to die because they asserted their rights.

This narrative is not one of many that remains to be written. That is not because each and every member of the Jewish resistance should not be called upon to write the story of his experience, but because there were so few who managed to fight and to save others. Each and every such story must be told because it is the record of the transformation of a people in the furnace of history. Jews have preached militancy and even fought to save themselves when that was possible throughout the two millennia of their exile. After each persecution, however, they returned to their former belief in human progress, and did little to change their own destiny. The end of the Second World War created a new Jew who no longer placed his faith in the liberal dream. Jews in Europe, led by those who had performed the feat of openly fighting against evil, cried out for an end to Jewish suffering in the present and offered their lives freely for that end. They proclaimed their unwillingness to accept anything less than a total rebirth of Jewry in its ancient homeland. In a mounting wave they struggled against the British to reach the Promised Land and to fight for the resurrection of the ancient Jewish nation. By their deeds in the diaspora they gave encouragement to the Yishuv in Israel to enter the battlefield. By refusing to settle for less, they made the creation of a sovereign Jewish state inevitable.

The deeds of men like Mietek Gruber have changed the destiny of the Jewish people and created history. If today Jews understand that there is a fate worse than war, it is a direct result of the actions of the heroes who fought a battle more difficult than any faced by a regular army. The story of Samuel (Mietek) Gruber and those like him who did battle in the wilderness of eastern Europe is the answer to the problem of the Jewish tragedy.

I

Captured by the Germans

In September 1939, war came to Poland.

Within hours of the start of the fighting, I was in the army at Nove Sanz, not far from Cracow. A week later, my outfit was transferred to Zacopane, a lovely resort in the Carpathian mountains near the Slovak border. Nestled in a thickly wooded region, Zacopane was completely isolated from the world, and though everyone could see that we soldiers were digging ditches, the wealthy vacationers were not even aware that war had broken out—until one morning they awoke to the spatter of German gunfire from across the border.

Our officers had vanished and we were left under the command of one lone sergeant. In the distance, to the south, were the idyllic, blue-topped mountains of the Carpathian range, through which—though I did not know it at the time—the German armies were pouring in from Slovakia.

In the early morning, some of us wandered down the hill toward a little stream. As we turned back toward our base, I heard our sergeant shouting at the top of his voice. At the same time, there was a burst of gunfire to the left and in the rear. I could not see much because by now I was in one of the trenches I had helped dig, but I was able to make out our sergeant on top of the hill, waving frantically. As I looked at him, a shell burst between us and his head was blown off. What was left of him vanished in a cloud of earth, smoke, and dust.

The air was filled with shouts and with the whistling whine of bullets. Bursts of machine-gun fire came from the top of the hill. The noise was moving rapidly across to my right, and I could see figures, obviously German soldiers, running in all directions. All the soldiers in my brigade had simply evaporated and I found that I was alone. Once again, a shell burst, this time directly above my head. I dived head first into the trench as if it had been a swimming pool. Dragging my rifle, I wriggled along to my left towards the stream and the trees of a nearby apple orchard. The firing grew louder and now seemed to come from the top of the hill behind me. I looked to my left. In the distance, beyond the trees, was a country road. I caught glimpses of metal shining in the sunlight and heard the rumble of trucks. The firing grew louder. I felt a powerful blow on my right shoulder; the impact threw me flat on the ground and knocked my rifle from my hand. I looked around to see what had hit me, but could see nothing.

The top of the hill was now empty of troops and the sound of the gunfire was receding. I saw the red roof of a farmhouse in the trees and crawled towards it.

My right arm was numb and my hand useless. I picked up my rifle with my left hand. By this time I was bleeding profusely and feeling faint, but I managed to stagger to the back entrance of the farmhouse. I banged on the door. A young woman opened. "Go away .... please!" she cried. But when she saw my blood-stained uniform and my white face, her kindness got the better of her. She gave a little gasp and pulled me in. When the door closed behind me, I found myself in a kitchen, and I promptly collapsed against the wall. The woman went off to one side and moments later returned with a basin filled with water and some clean white linen. With an efficiency that surprised me, she stripped off my uniform jacket and cleansed my wound. Then she made a compress, pressed it against my shoulder to stop the bleeding, then tied it tightly in place. She was badly frightened. "What if the Germans come and search this house? If they find you, they'll kill you, and they'll kill me, too, for giving shelter to a Polish soldier. My husband's at the front. Only God knows whether he's still alive. And my children are at school. So what do I do with you?"

I assured her that, if the Germans came, she would come to no harm. After all, I was wounded; they could hardly say that she had been hiding a fighting man in her house.

She took my rifle and put it into a corner. As she did so, there was a loud crash against the front door, and it flew wide open. There stood a huge German officer with a revolver in his hand. Other German soldiers were running up the stairs, their boots making a deafening noise. The officer pointed his gun at me. I raised my good arm and began to speak to him in German.

"You can see that I'm wounded," I told him. "My right arm is broken. I was on the hill over there when I got hit. This young woman who is treating my wound is a complete stranger to me. . . ."

The German laughed. "Well, my friend, for you the war is over!" he chortled. He seemed to be in high spirits; perhaps he was glad to have found someone who could speak German. Two of his men marched into the kitchen and reported that the rest of the house was empty. With great calm and presence of mind, the young woman pointed out my rifle in the corner, and then asked whether she could give the men some coffee, bread and eggs. The officer laughed again. "Sure, if you'll be quick about it." He tossed my rifle to one of his men and turned back to me, treating me as if I were a comrade-in-arms instead of an enemy soldier. He and his men had been marching for hours, he said, and could use some good food. They ate the bread and the eggs and even offered me a bite now and then. After they had finished eating, the officer looked at my shoulder. "We will get you to a hospital," he said. "We've taken over the hospital in Nove Sanz."

A few minutes later, I was led out of the house and put on a cart in which there already were some other wounded Polish soldiers. The German officer was still in a splendid mood. He informed us that the entire northern part of Poland had been occupied by the German forces and that Warsaw was surrounded and would probably fall to the Germans in a few hours. "Just a few more days," he declared, "and the war will be all over."

My own war had scarcely begun.

13

II

Back to Civilian Life

I had always had the makings of a good soldier. In 1936 I had been drafted into the Polish army where I received my basic training, eventually reaching the rank of corporal in the 54th Tarnopol Brigade. My immediate superiors thought that I should make the army my career and recommended me for officers' training, but it was Polish government policy to discourage Jews from joining the officer corps. I realized that, in view of the anti-Semitism that prevailed, my prospects for promotion were non-existent. Therefore, when my year of compulsory service was over in 1938, I returned to Podhajce, my home town, which today is part of the Soviet Union. My family consisted of my parents, one brother and three sisters. My father, a builder in Lemberg, had come to Podhajce to do some construction work; there he met and married my mother. The town derives its name from the great forest *(gaye* or *haje)* amidst which it first arose. As the town grew, the woods were largely chopped down, giving way to fields and gardens.

Jews first settled in Podhajce as far back as the early 1500's and helped spark the town's economic and cultural growth. During the later 1600's, the Jews of Podhajce fought side by side with their Polish neighbors against Tatar and Turkish invaders. Following the partition of Poland, Podhajce became part of the vast Austro-

Hungarian monarchy, remaining under the rule of the Habsburg emperors until the end of World War I and the establishment of the Polish republic.

Jewish community life in Podhajce down to recent times was that of the East European *shtetl* with its rabbis and scholars, merchants and craftsmen, and its internecine quarrels between the Orthodox and the non-observant, the Zionists and the assimilationists.

Almost immediately on my return, I had a painful personal encounter with anti-Semitism. Before I could settle down to civilian life and go back to my former job I had to get the proper identification papers from the local authorities. When I presented myself at the town hall I found, much to my surprise, that an old classmate of mine from my Lwow days was sitting behind the issue-desk. Kowalchyk and I had been good friends in high school and we had both dated the same girls. The fact that the girls he went out with were often Jewish never had seemed to present any kind of problem to him at that time.

"Fancy meeting you here, Kowalchyk," I greeted him cheerfully. "Can you issue me with a set of identification papers?"

Kowalchyk gave no sign that he recognized me.

"Kindly go out again, please, and shut the door behind you," he replied. "You're supposed to knock on the door and wait for me to tell you to come in. Then you must address me as you would any other Polish official. Remember, I'm now an official of the Polish government and you're only a Jew."

As I left the town hall, I had known that I had had enough of Poland. Since I had been eighteen I had wanted to go and make a new life for myself in Palestine but, due to the British restrictions on immigration, I had not received a permit. Now, following this first brush with prejudice from a schoolmate and fellow countrymen after giving loyal service to the Polish army, I decided to try to immigrate to the United States. My oldest sister had already been living there for ten years, and she and her husband seemed to be doing well and would sometimes send a few dollars to my parents. She also often wrote me letters urging me to leave Poland and join her in New York. She even sent me an affidavit for the American consul in Warsaw guaranteeing to support me in the United States until I found employment so that I should not

15

become a public charge. To obtain an American visa, however, I required an additional affidavit from another American citizen, but since I did not know anyone else in the United States, that exit route was cut off.

My thoughts then turned to Palestine and I entered a *hakhshara,* which was a training farm in which young people received training for pioneer life. My "kibbutz" was near the city of Chodorov where, for well over a year, my fellow trainees and I lived together and worked at wood-chopping and in a sugar refinery to prepare ourselves, so we thought, for what we might be required to do in Palestine. This preparation, combined with the basic army training I had received while in military service, was to prove an invaluable asset to me in my future life as a leader of the partisans in the Polish forests and villages.

Some of my *hakhshara* friends tried to get to Palestine "illegally"—that is, without the official British immigration permit. But not all of them were successful; a few were caught by the British and turned back.

Then the war broke out, effectually putting an end to all these projects.

III

In a German Hospital

"Just a few more days," the friendly German officer had said, "and the war will be all over."

Although he and his men were treating me with the courtesy due a prisoner of war, his words were hardly a comfort. It was an unseasonably warm day, and I was weak from pain and loss of blood. Besides, there was something that my captors did not know: I was not only an enemy soldier. I was also a Jew.

It took us almost four hours to make the short trip to Nove Sanz. Our little procession of horse-drawn carts moved at a snail's pace because the highway was jammed with German soldiers and vehicles, and with hundreds of farm wagons piled high with refugees and their belongings. The sides of the road were lined with soldiers and country folk, sitting on the ground and staring dumbly at the dismal scene.

By the time we reached Nove Sanz, I was barely conscious. Since the hospital was already filled to capacity, we were told to lie down on the ground in the hospital courtyard. Some German orderlies came out of the building and looked us over. After what seemed hours, I was placed on a stretcher and carried inside to the examination room. It turned out that my wound was quite serious.

My shoulder had been damaged at the joint so that I could neither raise my right arm nor move the fingers of my right hand. After the medico had finished examining me, I was carried into the ward, put to bed and given a shot of morphine. But at least I was alive.

The next morning I was awakened early for a more thorough examination by two doctors—a German army doctor and a civilian doctor, a short, squat Czech who was acting as the army man's assistant and interpreter. "This patient should be sent to Cracow for surgery," the German doctor said. I was taken to an X-ray room which was already crowded with other patients when I got there, so that several hours went by before I was returned to my ward.

Later that day, at suppertime, the Czech doctor suddenly materialized at my bedside. He bent over me, pretending to examine me once again, and whispered into my ear, "You know they're willing to send anybody who wants it to Cracow for further treatment. But whatever you do, don't ask them to send you, because they're killing all the Jews there. You just stay here and I'll see that nothing will happen to you."

He had me transferred into another ward where he was personally in charge and able to look after me himself.

I spent the next two months in that hospital. Everyone in the ward was friendly. All the patients were considered to be Polish prisoners of war and given courteous treatment. No attempt was made to single out the Jews among the patients or to treat them as anything else but Polish POW's. The orderlies and nurses kept us up to date on the latest news. There had been a savage battle for Warsaw; the civilians had fought alongside the soldiers to defend their city. In the end, the Luftwaffe had gone into action and reduced the city to flames and rubble. We were also told that the armored divisions of General Guderian, one of the ablest German field commanders, had moved east to Brest-Litovsk and had met the Russians head on. At first it was thought that the Russians would engage Guderian's forces in battle, but then it became apparent that the Russians and the Germans had agreed to divide Poland between themselves. The Polish government, it was said, had given up and fled to Rumania.

After just twenty-nine days of fighting, Poland had disappeared from the map of the world. Its western sector had been gobbled up by the armies of Adolf Hitler; its eastern sector, by the forces of Josef Stalin. What, I wondered, would become of us Jews now? Podhajce was in the Russian zone and, so far as I knew, my father and mother were still there, safe from the Germans, for the time being. My Czech doctor tried his best to reassure me. Since my home town had become part of Russia, and Russia and Germany were thick as thieves, I would no longer be considered a prisoner of war but a friendly alien. He was sure, he said, that I would soon be repatriated and reunited with my family.

In the meantime, my arm had become much better; I was able to move my fingers again. A nurse, under the direction of my little Czech doctor, massaged my shoulder every day and slowly swung my arm in circles. The treatment was painful but it helped me regain the use of my right arm.

IV

A Jewish POW in Germany

My Czech doctor was obviously skilled in his profession, but his predictions for my immediate future turned out to be wrong. After I had been in the hospital for about two months, the Germans rounded up all the prisoners of war and put us aboard special trains. When we asked where we were going, we were informed that we would be taken west, to Germany.

After a journey of two days we arrived at our destination: Stalag 13A in Langwasser, a suburb of the infamous city of Nuremberg, scene of Hitler's mammoth Nazi party rallies.

On our very first day at Stalag 13A, we ceased to be Poles and were classed as "Aryans" and Jews instead. At morning roll call, all the Jewish prisoners of war were ordered to step out of their lines and identify themselves. Most of the Jewish POW's obeyed at once. I, however, must admit that I was in no hurry to step forward. My "Aryan" fellow POW's standing on either side of me had been my friends; back at the hospital, they had been in the habit of asking me to divide their food rations among them and to act as arbitrator in their quarrels. But now, as we stood together in line for roll call, my friends seemed to have forgotten about those days. Instead of protecting me, they pushed me out of line to make sure that my Jewish identity would not be overlooked.

20

The Jewish POW's were moved to separate barracks which were, in fact, not barracks at all but huge canvas tents. Each tent sheltered about 70 men. We were not given cots but had to sleep on the bare ground without any blankets.

The Germans assigned us Jews to some rather odd outside labor details. Only a few days after our arrival at Stalag 13A, we were taken to the vast open-air stadium in Nuremberg where on certain red-letter days several thousands sat on bare stone tiers to listen to the rantings of their Fuehrer. The day before, it seemed, there had been a party rally and the stadium still bore traces of the event. We, the "Jew pigs," were assigned the task of cleaning up after the latest rally of Hitler's master race elite.

In was now mid-December, and the winter cold had set in full force. Lying on the frozen ground with only my uniform coat as a cover, my arm got worse again and I began to have trouble moving it. On one occasion, as I marched off with my labor detail, the German sergeant in charge called me to task for not swinging my right arm in proper marching fashion. I showed him my certificate from the hospital in Nove Sanz stating that I had been wounded and partially disabled, but the sergeant remained unimpressed. The next time he saw me with my right arm in the wrong position, he yanked me out of line and knocked me to the ground. This happened three times before the sergeant finally understood that I had not been malingering and mumbled a few undistinguishable words. I was lucky that we Jewish POW's were then under orders of the regular German army; unlike their counterparts in the notorious SS, the members of the *Wehrmacht* were mostly older men who still observed the rudiments of human decency.

Early in 1940 we, the Jewish POW's, were transferred, again by train, to Stalag 8 in Ludwigsburg. This camp was a vast improvement over Stalag 13A in that we now were quartered in regular wooden barracks instead of canvas tents. Shortly thereafter, we were moved once more, this time to the German air force base at Minsingen, not far from the French and Swiss borders.

Since I could do no heavy work, I was assigned to kitchen duty. One morning I was ordered to prepare the coffee for breakfast. This was the first time I had ever seen granulated sugar. Back home in Podhajce we had used only sugar loaves, from which we had chopped off chunks as we needed them. In Minsingen, my lack of experience with granulated sugar had unfortunate results. I sweetened the Wehrmacht's coffee with salt instead of sugar. The German overseers suspected me of deliberately seeking to sabotage the war effort. Once again, I had reason to be glad that the *Wehrmacht,* rather than the SS, was in charge of our camp. Had it been the SS, I probably would have been gunned down on the spot.

The only instances in which even the *Wehrmacht* singled out Jews for special punishment were those in which a Jewish POW attempted to escape. Since Minsingen was so close to the border of neutral Switzerland, a number of prisoners tried to make a getaway. If an "Aryan" POW was caught in the act, he received a stern lecture and was then sent back to his barracks. But if the prisoner was a Jew, he was executed by a firing squad.

So the winter passed. It was spring again, the spring of 1940, and as the weather became warmer, the war, which had been at a virtual standstill all winter long, picked up again. The Germans seized Norway and Denmark and attacked Holland. When we heard the news over the radio and from the guards, we came to instant new life. We were sure that the Germans would now get a trouncing from the vaunted French army. But in a matter of weeks our illusions were shattered. France surrendered and Hitler was the undisputed master of the European continent.

Toward the end of 1940 we heard rumors that Jewish POW's whose homes were in the Russian zone of Poland would shortly be repatriated in return for the release of Poles from the German zone of Poland who had been captured by the Russians.

Minsingen was visited by officials of the International Red Cross. I was interviewed by one of the officials who gave me my official Red Cross number. I remember it to this day; it was 30189. I wrote a letter to my family. After what seemed an endless time of waiting, I received an answer from my younger sister. My father, she wrote, was working for the Russian occupation authorities in the city, but he had become very old and ill and lived only for the day when he would be able to see me again.

Odd though it may seem, some of the trivia of daily life keep their meaning even in a prison camp. Knowing how much my sister had always admired my thick, dark hair, I wrote to her that the camp authorities had given me a crew cut, and that this had not exactly served to enhance my appearance. Her reply was: "It's good they only cut off your hair because I'm told that others have had their heads cut off. So be happy you still have your head on your shoulders." I don't know how our letters ever passed censorship; the only explanation I can offer is that, at the time, Germany had not yet gone to war with Russia.

V

Back in Poland

In January, 1941, the camp authorities announced that all the Jewish POW's from the Russian zone of Poland would be repatriated. We were put aboard a train which, indeed, was bound for points east. But instead of being taken to the border between the German and Russian zones, we were deposited in yet another prison camp, this one in Gerlice (Goerlitz), German Silesia. Here, for the first time, we met POW's from Western Allied countries, including soldiers from France and India. I myself saw how the Germans attempted to question one of the Indian prisoners. But the Indian was a proud man and spat into the Germans' faces.

A month later, in February, 1941, we had to board yet another train. This time, our destination was the ghetto of Lublin. At the Lublin railroad station we had our first encounter with the SS, who met our train, accompanied by huge, vicious-looking dogs. We marched off the train in a long, straight line with heads held high like proud soldiers, not meek Jews about to be led to the slaughter. Clearly, however, our SS welcoming committee did not like our attitude, for they began to beat us and set their dogs on us. "You're not soldiers, you know!" they shouted. "You're just Jewish swine, and don't you forget it!"

24

Our SS escorts took us to Lipova Street No. 7 where we were assigned to barracks which had once served as stables for cavalry horses. Our bunks of rough, unfinished wood were arranged along the walls in three tiers. There were neither blankets nor bedspreads. During our first week in Lipova Street, we were awakened every morning by the clatter of a horse's hooves on the cobbled street outside. The rider of the horse was an SS officer by the name of Dolf. Anyone still asleep when Dolf entered the barracks was shot at once; so was anyone too sick or weak to get up. Now there was no longer any pretense of our being Polish prisoners of war under the protection of the regular German army; we were simply Jews, interned in a special section of the Lublin ghetto under the command of the SS.

I was in Company 6, Barracks 6. Our group of POW's was soon joined by other Jews who had been rounded up from the ghetto proper—mechanics, artisans and other skilled workers who had helped put up our barracks and were now working for the German army. The commandant of our camp was a tall husky German named Riedel. He had a loud, raspy voice and little blue eyes sunk in fatty flesh which never showed any expression other than restrained fury. However, the Germans were not about to kill us; they needed us as slave laborers. Because of my injured arm, I was assigned to "inside" labor details. Most of the others, however, worked on "outside details," which meant that they left the ghetto every morning to perform their tasks under the supervision of the SS and returned to the ghetto only at night. Some of them were fortunate enough to meet Poles outside who were willing to engage in barter trading with the ghetto inmates, and so, from time to time, we received meat, bread, or scarce badly-needed articles of clothing such as good, sturdy shoes.

We got bread and other little comforts also from Jews who lived elsewhere in the Lublin and who came to visit us in our barracks from time to time. From them we learned that, several weeks before our own arrival in Lublin, another group of Jewish POW's, numbering over 1,000, had arrived. The SS had summarily turned them over to the Jewish Council which managed the affairs of the ghetto under the watchful eyes of the German overlords, and ordered the committee to feed the new arrivals. When the representatives of the committee protested that the ghetto was already on starvation rations and was in no position to provide food for another 1,000 men, the SS officer flew into a rage and marched the prisoners out of the ghetto in the direction of Lubartov, a little to the east of Lublin. But most of the prisoners never got that far. Anyone too weak to keep marching was summarily shot and left lying on the highway where they had fallen. By the time the sorry procession, escorted by SS men, reached Parczew, a suburb of Lublin, the group had shrunk to less than 100: nine out of every ten prisoners had been killed or had died on the way. At the time there still were some Jews in Parczew who shared their own meager food rations with these unfortunates. When the Jews in the Lublin ghetto heard what had happened to the POW's whom they had refused to take in, they resolved that such a tragedy should never occur again if they could possibly help it. That was why they were anxious to help us in every way they could.

Not long after our arrival in Lublin, the SS authorities announced that three of our group of POW's had been caught trying to escape from the ghetto. As a consequence, the SS routed us all from our bunks in the middle of the night and led us out, half naked, into the snow-covered street. We were ordered to take off our shoes. The Germans left us standing barefoot in the snow for two hours, during which we had to listen to a lecture from two German Jewish *kapos,* Simon and David. *Kapo* was a concentration camp term for prisoners, Jewish or otherwise, who acted as "trustees," working for the Nazi taskmasters, Many *kapos* were noted for the cruelty with which they treated their victims. Now Simon and David informed us that if anyone else in our group were to attempt to escape, he would be shot summarily, and that ten or twenty others would also be put to death for his crime.

At the end of two hours, we were ordered to return to our barracks. Next to each door and window there were SS men swinging leather whips. Anyone who passed too close to them received a lashing. I managed to get to the door unharmed. The man in front of me had broken down in sobs; he was begging the Germans not to whip him because he had a wife and children who, he hoped, were still alive somewhere. "So what?" the SS man retorted. "I also have a wife and children, but I have to spend my time guarding you, you stinking Jewish pig," and he whipped him.

Somehow, I escaped the SS man's whip.

This incident taught us a lesson, but it was not the one which the SS men had sought to impress upon us. Their brutality, instead of discouraging our attempts to escape from the ghetto, forced us to the realization that there was no other way out. We were determined that the next attempt would not be made by isolated individuals but as part of a carefully laid plan, and we were also determined that it would be successful.

As time went on, the Germans became more cruel. Before long, not a day went by without Jews being killed in the ghetto. The *Judenrat* (Jewish communal council acting as a liaison body between the Germans and the Jews) was supposed to carry out the orders of the Nazi officials. Most of the members of the council were elderly people who had enjoyed positions of esteem in Lublin's Jewish community before the war. One day they refused to obey some monstrous order passed to them by the ghetto commandant. The next day they were assembled in the ghetto square and led out of the city. They were never heard from again. In their place, the Nazis appointed one Jew to act as their stooge: he was Szama Grajer, a young man in his mid-twenties who lorded it over us worse than a Nazi. Much later, after the orderly liquidation of the ghetto, which his cooperation had helped to facilitate, the SS summoned him, or so the story goes, and heaped commendations upon him:

"You've been a very good Jew, a great help to us! As a reward you'll be the last to go." With that, they put a bullet in his head.

Our group at Lipova Street No. 7 was organized into twelve barracks. Each of these had a leader who in turn was responsible to an overall "elder" appointed by the Germans. Our "elder" was a man named Fischer who did all he could to improve our situation. Fischer managed to escape and survive the war; he is now living in Israel. He and his assistant Wallach got their orders from the SS each day through they *kapos* Simon and David, who later were shipped off to Maidanek along with all the other Jewish inmates of the Lublin Ghetto.

For a time the Jewish prisoners of war in the barracks of Lipova Street No. 7 were treated with a modicum of courtesy not accorded the inmates of the ghetto proper. The idea was that Russia and Germany were allies, and that one day we might be released and

27

repatriated in exchange for prisoners held by the Russians. But on the night of June 22, 1941 our hopes for speedy liberation were dashed. All that night we were kept awake by the continuous rumble of tanks and trucks and the drone of planes flying overhead. When we demanded to know what was going on, we received no reply. Instead, we were harshly informed that the whole area had been fenced off by electrified wires and that we had better stay within bounds. We felt that, at any moment, our captors might turn around and finish us off. After two or three days we were handed the scraps of some Polish newspaper which informed us that the pact with Stalin was at an end, that the German army had penetrated deep into Russia and was, in fact, already approaching Moscow. Once again, the war had caught up with us.

VI

Love and Friendship

Despite our situation, which seemed hopeless, we young single men and women in the Lublin Ghetto quickly formed friendships. I was no exception. Separated from my own family, I quickly developed two emotional relationships, one with a man and one with a girl.

At the barracks on Lipova Street No. 7, we frequently ran into friends and acquaintances from the old days. One of the friends I met was Henry Szengut, a well-educated man in his mid-twenties with whom I had become friends at Stalag 13 A. He had been captured by the Russians, but after the Germans had occupied his home town, he was told that he would be "repatriated" in accordance with an agreement made when Russia and Germany still had been on speaking terms. The irony in Szengut's case, of course, was that the Germans did not regard him as a "returnee" but as a Jew, and sent him to Lipova Street No. 7.

What is particularly poignant about Szengut's fate is that, since he had always had socialist sympathies, the Russians had urged him not to endanger his life by accepting "repatriation," but to settle in Russia. He, however, had persisted in his wish to rejoin his family in the German zone. In the end, it was his family who survived—they are living in Israel today—while Szengut was to die among the partisan fighters.

With Szengut I enjoyed one of those rare male friendships, based on mutual consideration, respect, and a certain tough, unsentimental humor that is capable of extracting fun even from the grimmest situation.

At the ghetto I also met Sandowski, another acquaintance from my days at Stalag 13 A. It was Sandowski's wife Miriam who introduced me to a girl called Cesia Wrobel. My relationship with Cesia, as well as my friendship with Szengut, made life bearable for me during those months.

I first met Cesia at the Sandowskis when she came in, triumphantly bearing three eggs in her hand. She had done some business with Poles outside the ghetto, and the eggs were her trophies. Her eyes shone and her cheeks were flushed. She seemed very pleased with life just then. I found her laughter very engaging, but I think that what first attracted me to her was her smile.

Later, she told me that she and her mother had come to Lublin from Warsaw, thinking that Lublin would be safer. The horrors which this young girl had already seen had turned her hair grey—a poignant contrast with the happy, childlike smile that drew me to her.

Immediately after we had been introduced, Cesia and Miriam Sandowski rolled up their sleeves, broke the three precious eggs and set to work baking a cake. I could not take my eyes from Cesia's smooth, bare arms as she kneaded the dough.

Somehow the two women had managed to get hold of some coffee. So, after the cake was ready, we sat around, eating, drinking and talking, forgetting for a few hours the despair that surrounded us. Perhaps this even gave an edge to our laughter. I don't think any cake I have ever eaten since then has tasted quite so good as that concoction made with three eggs in the Lublin Ghetto.

Later, Miriam Sandowski put on a record (somehow the music-loving Sandowskis had managed to bring their ancient portable record player with them into the ghetto) and the four of us danced. As I held Cesia in my arms, I tried to remember the last time I had done such a normal thing. I knew I had to be back in the barracks by evening, but that was still a long way off. Cesia wrapped a piece of the cake into some brown paper and shyly handed it to me.

"When can I see you again?" I asked. "And where?"

Since there were neither shows nor night clubs in the ghetto, and certainly no idyllic scenery through which to stroll hand in hand, we kissed in the shadow of a bridge and clung to each other in broken-down doorways. We wandered through the streets for hours, arm in arm, under the menacing gaze of the Nazi guards.

The prisoners of war had been put to work in various SS-run enterprises—tailor shops, cobblers' shops, metal shops, electrical shops and construction units. I myself was still in "limited service" because of my wounded arm.

Sometimes the Germans would take me with them as their interpreter when they did their shopping. They did not mind leaving me on my own for hours. I would gladly have used the opportunity to escape but saw little sense in attempting to do so because I was not yet familiar with the locality and might well have been captured and shot.

Still, my job allowed me more freedom than other prisoners to come and go as I pleased, and I took full advantage of it to see Cesia as often as I could. It was the thought of Cesia, her sparkling eyes and infectious laughter, that made life worth living.

Cesia and I tried to live a normal life under abnormal conditions. We loved to fantasize about eloping and running away to the forest or to make plans about what we would do after the war. We would get married, buy a house, settle down, have a family...But this was only make-believe on our part, and we knew it.

One afternoon I saw that Cesia had been crying. This was not like her, for until then, she had always met me with a smile. I tried to make her laugh with our usual let's pretend games.

"After the war I'll buy you a ring. I'll take you out on the town. Cabaret, movies, we'll do them all. We'll dance to real live music. And we'll throw a party for everybody, all our friends in the ghetto. We'll get married and someday we'll take our children to the beach..."

"I've just seen the Germans take a group of children out into the ghetto square," said Cesia in a voice not her own. "I heard cries, and I heard shots, and I saw...I saw...one SS man snatch up a baby on the point of his bayonet and toss it up into the air, catch

31

it on his bayonet, throw it up into the air, and catch it on his bayonet again, And the baby—it...I don't ever want to have a child! Not ever!''

I tried to take her in my arms to comfort her. "It's no use pretending," she said. "I don't believe this war will ever end. At least not for us. Not for the Jews. I don't see any hope for the Jews at all. Look, they kill even the children, so what hope can there be? There's only now. That's all we have together. Come home with me today. I'd like you to see where I live. And to meet my mother.''

I went back with her to their cramped living quarters. Cesia's mother was a wispy emaciated woman, old before her time. Mother and daughter exchanged a few whispered words. Then the mother excused herself; she had to visit a friend, she said.

I was due back in the barracks at nightfall, but even though it meant risking my life, I stayed with Cesia that night. She clung to me, her whole body trembling with the memory of what she had seen, and we made love, as if we could shut out the war. But that was impossible.

Something told me we would have very little time together, and it turned out that I was right. But it was neither the Germans nor the war that parted us.

One morning, at roll call, our group was informed that we had been chosen for an important work project just outside Lublin, under the command of Dolf. We were to build a prison camp—for what purpose we could only surmise at the time. As it turned out, the Germans, notwithstanding their reputation for efficient planning, had chosen the worst possible site: it was swampland, and the barbed wire fences and steel towers we raised on one day had all but vanished into the ground by the time we returned to work the next morning. For some reason the Germans allowed us to go on in this way for several months until finally, in the late summer of 1941, they gave up and announced that the project would be moved to a more suitable terrain not far away. The name of the place where we built the camp was Maidanek, and hundreds of thousands of innocent human beings were to die in the gas chambers there. Most of those killed were Jews.

The first inmates of the camp, however, were not Jewish deportees but Russian prisoners of war, who had been taken during the first two weeks after the outbreak of war between Germany and the Soviet Union in June 1941. As soon as they arrived, they were put to work building barracks, because there were not enough barracks to house them all. Within weeks, the unfortunate Russians got sick with a high fever and they began to drop dead like so many flies. The rumor spread that the Germans had given them poisoned food; they had wanted to get rid of them quickly because these prisoners had not been ordinary Russian soldiers but hard-core members of the Communist party. Each day, the Germans would load the dead onto army trucks and order us, the Polish Jews—there was no longer any pretense that we were prisoners of war—to dig mass graves and bury them.

The fever that killed the Russians turned out to be typhus. In our weakened condition, our contact with the corpses brought about the inevitable result: hundreds of the ghetto inmates who had been working on the Maidanek site became infected. I too got sick.

In a matter of days, the disease had reached epidemic proportions. Thoroughly frightened, the Germans piled about 400 of us, more dead than alive, into army trucks and drove us from the camp site back into the Lublin ghetto. There, they took us to the big synagogue and dumped us on the wooden floor like limp rag dolls. The SS men then summoned the committee of Jews who formed the puppet government of the ghetto, and told them of our arrival. "You'd better do something about those brothers of yours," the Germans said to the ghetto committee. "We don't want them to infect our German soldiers."

Three weeks of hellish misery followed. Of the 400 who had been brought into the synagogue, 100 died. Strangely enough, the ones who had seemed the healthiest and strongest were the first to die. Those who had looked the frailest appeared to have more stamina. I was lucky. Miriam Sandowski heard of my plight from Cesia. One day she turned up at the synagogue with another ghetto inmate, a doctor. I recall that the doctor gave me an injection. Where he obtained the drug, or the syringe, for that matter, I will never know. The ghetto was desperately short of medical supplies. I remember that after the doctor had attended to me, he turned around and left the synagogue without a glance at any of the others lying on the bare wooden floor of the synagogue. At any rate, I survived.

When Cesia discovered that I was lyin⁰ in the makeshift synagogue hospital delirious with typhus she was distraught. She came to visit me almost every day with some home-concocted remedy. Once, I remember, she even brought me flowers. Where she got them I cannot imagine. But I am certain it was the anticipation of her visits, and her smile when she came, that made me rally and get better. Another frequent visitor during that period was my friend Henry Szengut.

Eventually I returned, along with the other convalescents, to our barracks at Lipova Street No. 7 for a few weeks of rest before being ordered back to work. One day Henry brough me a book. After he left, I opened it and, to my surprise, a piece of paper fell out from between the pages and dropped to the floor. I bent to pick it up. It was a half-finished note in Henry's handwriting, and it was addressed to Cesia. "Look, Gruber's better now," he had written. "You'll have to tell him some time. Wouldn't it be fairer to him if you told him the truth about us now?"

I lay back on my bunk bed, bathed in a cold sweat. I had considered Henry my best friend. The next day, when he came to see me again, I confronted him with the note. "This fell out of your book. Did you mean for me to read it?"

Szengut could not look me in the face but kept his eyes on the ground like a guilty schoolboy.

"Look, Szengut," I said, "we might as well get this straight. Cesia's my girl—or so at least I thought. What's going on between you and her?"

"Well," Szengut replied, "it's like this. You were ill. She was upset. We all thought you were dying and. . . ." There was no need for him to finish.

He offered to go with me to Cesia and ask her to choose between us. We both called on her in the little room she shared with her mother. It was my first visit anywhere after my illness and I remember that I was barely able to walk. I looked around the room where Cesia and I had been so happy. This time Cesia was not smiling. I reassured her that I would abide by her decision, whatever it was. We would all three remain friends, but friendship required all parties to be completely honest with one another.

She admitted that, while I had been ill, she had fallen in love with Henry, and he with her, but that neither of them had had the heart to tell me. They had wanted to wait until I was completely recovered, but had never intended that I learn the truth from anyone else but directly from them.

Cesia began to cry. "I can't understand how it happened. I was so unhappy. I thought you were dying. And I wanted to die too, I felt so alone, and then Henry made me feel that perhaps I could go on..."

I left her and Henry without a word. I could not bear to see her so unhappy. After all, who could tell how much time there still remained for them—or for any of us?

Szengut and I kept our promise. He and I remained good friends as long as he lived.

VII

The Storage Room

The day after my talk with Szengut and Cesia, my period of convalescence came to an abrupt end. Fischer, the Jewish "elder" to whom all the barracks leaders reported, wanted to see me. One of our men in the detail assigned for work outside the ghetto, in the storage room of a German military hospital, had escaped. He had to be replaced before the Germans could find out that one of their Jews had run away and take terrible revenge on the entire camp. I was still classed as sick so that my name appeared not on the workers' list but on a separate roster and I could be slipped into the man's place without the ruse being discovered.

The next morning I reported for work at the hospital. It was a *Sammelstelle* or receiving center to which wounded and battle-fatigued German soldiers were brought directly from the front lines. The hospital was not under the supervision of the SS, but of the regular German army, and the Jews assigned to duty at the hospital—there were about 20 of us from the camp—were given quarters in special barracks and lived under better conditions than they had in Lipova 7.

My job was to take the clothing and weapons of the new arrivals, label them and register them for storage. The articles would remain in the storage room until their owners had recovered and were sent back to the battlefront. One day a German officer asked me to "pad" my inventories of items returned to soldiers about to be discharged, and to let him have the articles. Eventually I found out that he was engaged in a thriving business selling the guns and uniforms of the wounded. He never gave me a penny for my troubles, and at first it did not occur to me to ask to be cut in on the deal. Perhaps I was not yet clever enough then.

But soon I became wise to what was going on. My German officer was not the only German in the racket, nor was I the only Jew involved. The only trouble was that the other Jews in the hospital detail kept putting their loot under my cot, and I became afraid that I might get caught without ever having received a penny for my pains. I therefore joined in the business with a vengeance. My "specialty" was not uniforms but weapons—pistols, side arms, ammunition and hand grenades. As I took the weapons from the new arrivals, I made a mental note of those patients who, obviously, would not go back to the front lines—soldiers who had lost an arm or a leg, or were badly shell-shocked and hence not likely to need guns again. These weapons I considered "safe." I turned them over to a co-worker, David Weingarten, who spirited them out of the hospital and got them to the underground movement. I'm still in touch with Weingarten from time to time. He survived the war and is now living in Israel.

Once each week—on Saturday night—I would go to the camp to pick up the bread rations of our hospital detail. Officially, the hospital was responsible only for our housing: the SS who ran the camp were expected to supply our rations. In fact, however, the Jews in the hospital detail always had plenty of bread because the German soldiers and the Polish prisoners of war stationed at the hospital had more than enough so that we never went hungry. But there was never enough bread to go around in the camp. Accordingly, instead of taking our ration back to the hospital, I would give it to my friends in Lipova 7. One day an SS man caught me in the act and took me to the headquarters of the new SS commandant at the camp, an officer named Mohrwinkel. Mohrwinkel gave me a good beating. but then let me go. Little did Mohrwinkel know that he had not seen the last of me. One generation later, on November 4, 1973, I was to face him from a witness box in a German courtroom where he was tried by the West German government as a Nazi war criminal.

37

VIII

Plans for Escape

During my weekly visits to the camp I met many comrades whom I had known for some time, and had long talks with them about what might be in store for us. I learned that the Germans were slowly emptying out the Lublin ghetto. Some of the inmates had been moved to another ghetto, Maidanek-Tatarski. There, they were told, they would be put to work for the duration of the war. They were given special identity cards and privileged treatment as "productive workers" actively engaged in aiding the German war effort. But only young people and individuals with special skills were fortunate enough to be sent to Maidanek-Tatarski. All the others, I was told, would eventually be deported to concentration camps, particularly Camp Maidanek, where Jews were being done to death by assembly-line methods.

At the hospital I made friends with some Polish prisoners of war, young men and women who were working as nurses or kitchen aids. One of them was a fellow named Pavel—I never learned his last name. He was a strange bird, different from the other Poles in his group. He always seemed preoccupied with his own thoughts. But he developed a liking for me and took me into his confidence, speaking to me quite frankly about whatever came to his mind.

"Listen," he whispered to me one day while we were working side by side mending German uniforms, "they'll kill all of you Jews—if not this year, then the next. No one will be left alive. You'd better try to escape." He told me that he had contacts with Polish partisan units which were hiding out in the forests just outside Lublin. The leader of one of the units, in fact, was a school friend of his. Also, Pavel explained, he knew that many Jews had already joined the partisans.

Back in the camp, I learned that Fischer, the camp "elder," his assistant, Wallach, and two of their friends, Jaeger and Kaganovich, had already established contact with the Polish underground forces. By that time, two separate underground resistance organizations had developed: the *Armja Ludowa,* known by its initials as A.L., and the *Armja Krajowa,* or A.K. *The Armja Ludowa* was a left-wing organization; the members of *Armja Krajowa,* on the other hand, were right wingers and had no particular liking for Jews. But because our small group—Fischer, his friends and I—had been in the Polish army at the outbreak of the war, some members of the A.K. were ready to talk to us despite the fact that we were Jews. They promised to give us trucks, rifles and ammunition, and to help us escape from the ghetto into the woods surrounding the city. One Sunday afternoon, when the entire ghetto population, 2,000 of us at the time, would be taken en masse outside the city for our weekly "delousing" session, the weapons and trucks would be waiting for us at a place to be agreed upon. There, we would break away from our SS escorts and make our bid for freedom.

The next week, at the hospital, I let Pavel in on the plans for our mass escape. He was skeptical about the whole thing. "It would be very nice if the A.K. would really help you get out," he said. "But frankly, I don't think you can depend on them. They might let you have some rifles and a few rounds of ammunition, but it won't be enough to fight the Germans. And even assuming that you got away from the SS men, the A.K. would pass the word on to other Germans and that would be the end of all of you. It wouldn't be the first time the A.K. would do that to the Jews. They've done it before. If you want to escape, do it in small groups, say about 20 or so at a time, so the A.K. won't notice and the Germans won't catch you. Once you have enough of your men out in the woods, you can organize an underground base and help bring out the rest."

"But what if one of the groups gets caught?" I asked. "Then it'll make no difference how many of us tried to escape. If the Germans catch even a dozen of us, they'll kill everybody that's still left in the camp.

"That's not a valid argument," Pavel retorted. "The Germans are out to kill all Jews, anyway. So save whomever you can. In that way some of you, at least, will stay alive."

The following Saturday, I reported Pavel's opinion to our men who had been negotiating with the A.K. Most of the men agreed with Pavel. They now realized that a mass getaway would almost certainly end in disaster. But by the same token, could we justify risking the lives of hundreds of innocent people, including women and children, who would have to remain behind indefinitely, on the very dubious chance that a few dozen might succeed in escaping to an uncertain fate in the woods? For months, we argued the question back and forth without being able to resolve it.

But one sunny morning in the summer of 1942 something happened in the camp that galvanized us into action. At the daily roll call, we were informed that Mohrwinkel had been relieved of his post as camp commander and had been succeeded by an SS officer named Schramm. Schramm had formerly been in charge of the camp electricians. We welcomed Schramm's promotion as a piece of unhoped-for good news. Schramm had been uniformly praised in the camp as one of the "good" Germans. The Jews who had been working under him had actually liked the man; they thought that perhaps Schramm was not really a Jew-hater at heart. But within moments after Schramm had mounted the reviewing stand in his new capacity, we were shocked into revising our judgment. One of the boys in our line made a sudden, innocent move. Schramm strode up to him, whipped his pistol from its holster and shot him on the spot.

Was brutality a catching disease? Or had Schramm been subjected to some sort of horrible brainwashing before he could qualify for his new responsibilities? Whichever had been the case, if sudden power could turn a man like Schramm, seemingly so easy-going and good-natured, into a cold-blooded killer like the rest of his comrades, what could we possibly have to lose by attempting to escape from the ghetto?

We decided to follow Pavel's advice, at least for a start. We sent out an advance guard of forty men, armed with rifles and ammunition. They were led by a dark-haired, handsome young man from Brzezany, a place near my home town—his name was Zeifer. Plans called for the men to set up a partisan base in the Yanow woods, outside Lublin, in a bunker prepared ahead of time by a team of Polish underground fighters.

Unfortunately, of the forty men of the advance guard who left for the woods only two survived to tell of the fate that had befallen the others. After completing their work on the bunkers, the Polish underground fighters had hidden out in the woods to await the arrival of our men. When our men had filed into the bunker, the Poles, who were supposed to be their allies against the Nazis, rushed out from their hiding places, threw hand grenades into the bunker they themselves had built, and opened fire on those inside. At the time the *Armja Ludowa,* the left-wing freedom fighters, blamed the rightist partisans, the *Armja Krajowa,* and spread abroad a story of how the "sons of the bourgeoisie" had killed forty "heroes." No one took the trouble to add that the forty "heroes" had been Jews. However, in the 1960's, under the Communist regime of Gomulka, it was revealed that one of the leaders of the *Armja Ludowa,* a man named Korczynski, had been tried in a Polish court on suspicion of murder.

IX

To the Woods

The loss of our 38 comrades left us shaken, but determined that our own time for escape had come, even if we were to die in the attempt. One day early in October, 1942, my friend Szengut, Cesia (who was now universally accepted as Szengut's girl), Sandowski and I met with two members of a Polish partisan unit to make plans for the escape of 22 Jews, including ourselves. Our meeting place was, strangely enough, a restaurant. In the midst of the ghetto and under the very noses of the SS, enterprising Jews had set up small eating places which offered black market delicacies and which were openly frequented even by the Polish police.

The two partisans had come well prepared, with maps and with promises of guides who would lead us out of the city to a safe place in the woods. We set the date: October 28, 1942, some time between dusk and seven o'clock in the evening. There would be two young Poles waiting for our group of 22 behind some trees at a certain spot in a suburb of Lublin. They would wait for us until seven. If something untoward befell and we would not be able to get there by that time, it would be our bad luck because the two Poles would not be able to wait for us beyond that hour.

Early on October 28, Jaeger, one of Fischer's friends, came to me at my place of work in the storage room of the German army hospital. He was very much upset. Kaganovich, who had been sent with a considerable amount of cash to buy rifles for us from his connections in the Polish underground, had met with bad luck. His Polish go-betweens had taken the money, but had not brought him so much as one pistol in return. What, Jaeger asked in near-despair, was the use of trying to escape without weapons? He was ready to call off the whole project.

But I was determined to let nothing stop us. I grabbed hold of Jaeger's jacket sleeve and said:

"I don't know about you, or the others, but I know about myself—I'm leaving. I have one revolver and a couple of rounds of ammunition. I'll meet the two Polacks outside the city and I'll wait there until seven. It's up to you, Jaeger, to see that the others come, too. But if they aren't there by seven, that'll be just too bad; I'll make it alone, then."

At about noon that day, I met Miriam and Cesia and told them Jaeger's bad news.

"I still think you ought to go," said Cesia. "If Henry and you make it to the woods, then just send me word and I'll come, too."

"But do you think a woman could survive such a life?" I asked dubiously.

"Well, a woman certainly can't survive here," she declared defiantly. "So that's settled. Can't you remember, Sam, when we used to talk of running away to the woods together? Well, here's our chance. I'm not missing it. You just get a message back to me when you're both settled, and I'll be sure to come. If it weren't for my mother, I'd come straight away." If Cesia had come, she might have been alive today.

During my last hours at the hospital, however, I very nearly fouled up everything because I insisted on having a second pistol, which I obtained in the usual way from the hospital's storage room. The victim of the theft was a German colonel, who had just arrived at the hospital with a slight wound in his leg. He seemed to be looking for something. I asked him whether he had lost anything. Yes, he said, he seemed to have misplaced his pistol. I said that it probably had already been tagged with his name and number, like all the other weapons brought in by wounded officers and men. I assured him that it would not be lost and that it would be duly returned to him whenever he was ready to leave the hospital. But the colonel still had misgivings; he had placed it on the counter only seconds ago. He knew we were efficient, he said, but how could the gun have been registered, labeled and put away in split-seconds? I told him that we were in the habit of working fast in the storage room. One did not leave weapons lying around unattended. I could hardly have told him that the pistol he was missing had already found a new home in my own belt.

The officer continued arguing and muttering under his breath for a few more minutes but, luckily for me, his heart was apparently not in it. He had caught sight of the food cart and hobbled painfully after it. Following his long train ride from the battlefront to the hospital, he was ready for a good meal.

Toward evening, I got hold of a little leather sack (also formerly the property of one of our patients), and sauntered into the hospital kitchen. Fortunately, no one was around just then. I filled my sack with a loaf of bread and some carrots—that was all the food I could find—and slipped out of the hospital. As I went out the door, I slapped my friend Pavel on the back and said to him, "See you later," for the benefit of anyone who might hear. Pavel lit a cigarette, smiled, and gave me a brief, knowing nod.

Once outdoors, I set out in the direction of the camp but soon turned off into an alley. By that time dusk had come and I was able to move unseen through alleys and roundabout side-streets to the meeting place among the trees, arriving there just as it was getting dark. Like sleek cats, the two Poles emerged from behind the trees and nodded to me. We stood in the shade and waited.

Six o'clock came and went. By six-thirty the two guides were getting restless. They would not be able to wait much longer, they told me, because they might be stopped by spies or by a German night patrol. I insisted on their waiting until the last minute. It was a good thing that I did.

At about five minutes to seven, a group of men emerged from the shadows. They stopped some distance away and cautiously looked up and down the quiet, tree-lined street. I gave a low whistle and they all came running over. I recognized Henry Szengut and the hulking figure of Kaganovich. Jaeger was there, too. There were eight other men I knew: Stefan Finkel, Zelazny Eisenberg, Cygan, Heiden (a young man from my own home town), Burstyn, Furman, Matros and Andreiev. The cause for their delay had been that at the last moment, the ghetto committee, who had been informed by Sandowski and Cesia of our plans, had insisted on sending along with the group a twenty-third comrade, a man, hardly more than a boy, who had escaped from Camp Maidanek that very day and had sought shelter in the ghetto. I never learned his name, but he was soon to figure prominently in our story.

Everyone was tense as we all shook hands and I introduced the two Polish partisans who were to act as our guides. Szengut gave me a little note from Cesia, wishing us luck and reminding us of my promise that we would send for her as soon as we could.

We moved off in groups of twos and threes, with the two Poles leading the way. By the time we have been walking fifteen minutes, it had become totally dark, and the sky was overcast. Soon we had left the last of the city's houses behind us and were walking along a railroad embankment that led to a small river. Across the river was the forest, and safety. At the river's edge the Poles stopped and explained that we would not be able to use the bridge because it was guarded by Germans. We would have to wade across the river. We were to take off our clothes, roll them into a bundle and carry them across on our heads. As for our shoes, they suggested that we tie the laces together and wear the shoes around our necks. Once across the river, we were not to stop and put our clothes on but keep moving across the open ground until we had reached the woods. It was not a pleasant prospect; the water was icy cold and there was a chill in the late autumn air. But our guides only laughed and said that the exercise would keep us warm. They had already begun to peel off their clothing. Some of our group were protesting that they could not swim, but our guides assured us that the river was fordable at this point. Urged on by the two Poles, we marched forward into the water, gasping and jumping up and down in the running stream. The river was not very deep or wide and we all reached the other side in short order, thoroughly chilled but safe and sound. We crawled up the bank, our bare feet sliding in the mud. Then we hopped and jumped across the cold, slimy turf and finally reached the shelter of the trees. There we hastily threw on our clothing, laughing and declaring that we now had been properly baptized for our new lives as freedom fighters. We were in high spirits as we started upon our journey into the unknown.

Led by our two Poles, we continued through the forest all night long. At dawn, we came to the edge of the forest and a small village. Near the village—its name was Yastkov—we met a group of girls who turned out to be Jewish and, like ourselves, fugitives from the Lublin ghetto. They had with them a towheaded Polish boy named Mikhael. He, too, had escaped from Lublin, but not because he had anything against the Nazis. He had fled the city because he was wanted there for petty larceny.

We asked our new friends whether there were any Germans in the vicinity. They told us that, indeed, there were. Near Yastkov, there was a labor camp with a large number of Jewish inmates. The Germans had put the Jews to work on a road construction project, and every morning, the Germans escorted the Jews to the work site. Though our entire arms supply at the time consisted of little more than the two pistols I had contributed, we decided to lie in wait for the Germans, pounce upon them when they came by, relieve them of their weapons and liberate the Jewish slave laborers.

Unfortunately, this was not our lucky day. The work detail did not come out that morning, nor the next day. Eventually, the Jews from the Yastkov camps were to join our ranks, but this did not happen until much later. Obviously we could not stay in Yastkov forever, waiting for the labor detail to turn up. Besides, we were still too close to Lublin and the SS guardians of the camp. We therefore bade good-by to the Mikhael and the young ladies and moved on.

After several hours we reached the Kozlowietzky forest. The place seemed ideal for setting up camp. The foliage was very thick, a good protection against possible raids by German patrols. There was even a stream of clean, ice-cold water close by. Kaganovich and I explored the surrounding area. Used as we were to the comforts of town life, the idea of sleeping out in the open exposed to wind and weather held no particular charms for us. Also, after the crowded life in barracks and ghetto we had become fearful of the wide open spaces. For a moment our courage, which the Nazis had been unable to shake, dissolved at the thought of forsaking civilization—such as it was—and living like the animals. Would we be able to adapt? It was impersonal Nature which was now the chief threat. The wind made weird noises as it whistled through the treetops, and we had to become accustomed to the cries of the animals who shared the forest with us. Our two Poles told us that there were wild hogs and even wolves in the area, but they assured us that these seldom came near human beings, that they were at least as much afraid of us as we were of them. We certainly hoped that our guides were right.

The wind was biting cold but the trees afforded us some shelter from its icy breath. From time to time the sounds of the night were broken by what seemed like piercing shrieks. One night it seemed so close and frightening that some of us got up and went out to see where it came from. Was there another person nearby, perhaps wounded and in pain? The screaming stopped. We waited, listening in utter silence.

Just as we thought we would go back to our camp site, there it was again, that fearful shriek; this time it seemed to come from directly overhead. We looked up, but all that we could see against the night sky was the waving tops of the trees and a few scurrying clouds. Now the shriek appeared to come from the very top of a giant tree. Finally Andreiev, a good climber (and a great show-off to boot), said he would soon find out. He had swung himself into the lowest branches of the tree, when the shriek came again, followed this time by a drawn-out whine. Andreiev nearly fell out of the tree but, bolstered by our shouts of encouragement from below, he climbed higher, slowly vanishing behind the thick foliage. Nothing daunted Andreiev as long as enough people were watching. After what seemed hours of suspense the long, eerie whining sound came once more, and Andreiev seemed to be right in the middle of it. Then we heard the sound of wood being chopped.

"Oh, Andreiev has his tomahawk!" someone laughed.

Andreiev had gotten hold of a small ax and cherished it like a treasure. He kept sharpening it all the time, and whenever he had nothing else to do, he would practice throwing it as he had seen the Indians do in Wild West movies. Indian-style, he fondly called it his "tomahawk." Now he was putting it to practical use. Suddenly a heavy bough fell out of the tree and dropped to the ground, Andreiev following close behind. After he had picked himself up and established that no bones had been broken, he pointed excitedly to the bough.

"That's it. That's what was making the noise!" He showed us a split end. "It was hanging from the trunk, by this part here, split—see—and whenever the wind blew through the tree this branch was swinging back and forth and rubbed against the trunk. That's what made that awful screeching sound. That's all it was—nothing more. Would you believe it?"

It was hard to believe at first, but Andreiev must have been right, because the screeches were heard no more.

X

The Fugitives Organize

Our worries eased for the moment, we organized our band of fugitives for efficiency and safety. We split into two groups, one led by Kaganovich, the other by me. We began by adopting Polish names. We depended entirely on Polish peasants for food and supplies, and we knew that if the peasants were even so much as to suspect us of being Jews, they would never give us anything. I myself took the name of Mietek; this was a typical Polish name, but I got the idea from Munyo, the pet name by which my family had called me at home.

Our two groups alternated every night foraging nearby farmsteads for food. Kaganovich or I, accompanied by our men and by one of the Polish guides, would pick out a farmhouse and head for it. The Pole would knock on a window.

"What do you want so late at night?" was the usual greeting from the farmer inside. We were a wild-looking crew, but we would try to put our hosts at ease immediately. We did not come to kill anyone, we explained. And then we launched into a long speech; we were Polish partisans, fighting to make our homeland free again. To this end, we had set up a camp in the woods, from where we launched sudden attacks on the German enemy. Could we have some water or milk, and perhaps a little food to keep us going for the next few days?

49

As time went on, we became a little bolder and began to solicit clothing as well. When we had left Lublin, the weather had still been fairly mild during the daytime and so, in order not to arouse suspicion, we had not wanted to carry coats with us through the streets of the city. but now, with winter approaching, we were badly in need of heavy wraps. Besides, our sweaters, shirts and pants were hanging from us in tatters. Since proper clothing is an important part of good morale in any disciplined band of underground fighters, we started combing the farmhouses also for old army uniforms.

After we had been in the forest about two weeks, our two Polish guides announced that they were quitting. "Listen, men," they explained, "you can't be partisan fighters with not even one rifle. We need serious weapons. Without that, we're dead ducks. Unless you can find a way of getting us some weapons, fast, we'll wash our hands of the whole thing."

We agreed that something had to be done, and quickly. We called a joint meeting of our two groups and decided to send the two Poles back to Lublin for weapons. For this purpose, we gave them whatever cash and valuables, including wrist watches, which we still had on us. We saw no reason not to trust the two underground fighters. They left us at twelve that night, laden with our last possessions and that was the last we ever saw or heard from them.

We were now completely on our own, a partisan unit, as we saw it, or a band of gangsters, as the Germans called our kind.

Before long, winter was upon us in earnest, and, once again, trouble struck. The boy from Maidanek who had joined our group in Lublin came down with a high fever. His escape from the death camp had been nothing short of miraculous. A peasant had entered the camp and proceeded to pile dung onto his empty horse-drawn wagon. Our new friend had jumped onto the wagon and buried himself in the dung. When the wagon lumbered out of the camp, it did not occur to any of the German sentries that underneath all the dung, there was a Jewish boy about to regain his freedom. But the hardships and utter exhaustion had taken their toll, and we strongly suspected that our young refugee had caught typhus. We built him a little dugout, covered with a primitive shade we had made from fallen branches. There, we hoped, he would be protected and also safe from being discovered while the rest of us went out in search of new farmhouses to forage. All odds seemed to be against him; he was nothing but skin and bones, and there was no way of getting him medical help. Yet, eventually, he recovered.

After the boy had regained his strength sufficiently to be able to travel with us, we moved to another part of the forest, for we had just about exhausted the good will of the peasants we had been soliciting for food and clothing. The time had come to seek out other places where we were not yet known. Our friend Pavel had told us that the forests surrounding Lublin were full of underground fighting units, including many Jews. But we were sadly disappointed; the only other human beings we encountered in the woods were Poles who were hiding out in the forest because they were on the wanted list as thieves or murderers. They moved about in twos and threes; for food, they hunted down small wild animals. They supplemented this monotonous diet with whatever they were able to steal from farmhouses; most of their loot consisted of liquor.

After marching all night and through most of the day that followed, we arrived in a small wooded area which, according to the detailed map our partisan friends had given me in Lublin, was the Garbowsky forest, east of the city. We had not been there long when we became aware of noises and then the sound of human voices not far away. At first we thought that these were peasants, ready to go home from their work in the woods. But when we came to the clearing we saw a whole camp of men who did not look in the least like Polish peasants. Some of them were carrying weapons.

"Amcha*?" I ventured. This was the Hebrew greeting by which Jews have identified themselves to each other for centuries.

"Amcha," they replied, and within moments we were engulfed in embraces, back-slappings and a deluge of questions. They told us that they had come from the town of Markuszow, and that almost all the Jews of Markuszow, young and old, men, women and children, had been able to flee before the Nazis could have caught them and put them into a concentration camp.

To our amazement, the men told us that about 100 other refugees from Markoszow, older men, women and children, were hiding out in various sectors of the forest, safe while they, the

*Literally: "Your (i.e. God's) people."

51

younger men in the camp, went out to get them food and clothing from the farmhouses. Unlike us, they had a fairly adequate supply of weapons, including a machine gun.

After a while, they introduced us to two Gentiles, Tolka and Mikoi. These turned out to be Russian army officers, who had been interned in a German POW camp in Lubartow, but had managed to escape. Tolka had already been hiding out in the woods for some time and made contact with a Polish underground base. When he and his comrade, Mikoi, had come upon the Jewish refugees from Markuszow, he had tried to organize them into an efficient fighting force to attack the Germans, but, much to his disappointment, he had not been very successful. He said that he was glad, at long last, to meet Polish Jews like our men who looked and behaved like well-trained soldiers. He begged me to lend him some of my best fighters to help him train those with whom he had been blessed. I lent him Jaeger, Cygan, and one or two others—which ones, I do not remember now.

Tolka was anxious for us to meet the Polish underground leader whom he had contacted. Accordingly, Tolka and I, accompanied by a Markuszow man named Sever Rubinstein, set out for the village of Garbow, where the underground leader, Genek Kaminsky, had set up headquarters in a fairly large house.

Genek, as he instructed us to call him, had been a member of the Communist party before the war. But for the time being, party considerations were secondary; the task immediately at hand was to help rid Poland of the Nazi plague. He asked us a few brief questions. Then he took over the meeting. In order to cease being mere fugitives and to begin the active struggle against the Germans, we would have to get more weapons, he said. There were plenty of peasants who had veritable arsenals in their homes—ammunition, rifles and even machine guns which the menfolk had brought home with them in their helter-skelter retreat from the Germans back in 1939. Why not see what we could get from these peasants?

We followed Genek's suggestion with dispatch. Some of the peasants gave us a little difficulty. They belonged to the *Armja Krajowa,* and had found out that our group and the people from Markuszow were Jews. As far as they were concerned, the Jews were little better than the devil. The result was that we had to administer a few good beatings to those peasants before we could get any weapons at all. But in some instances my one pistol, brandished with the proper gestures into a slow-witted peasant's face, was sufficient. Our forays into the countryside near the Garbowky Forest yielded us a grand total of ten rifles and about a dozen rounds of ammunition.

Clearly the farmhouses at the edge of the forest were not rich sources of military supplies. Therefore, we decided to send one of our men to Lublin to "organize" some weapons. Our choice fell upon Stefan Finkel, who looked so utterly like a Pole that one was hard put to think of him as a Jew. We instructed him to visit our friends who were still working at the German military hospital in Lublin, where guns and other weapons of wounded German soldiers could be obtained with ease. Also, we now had found the right time and opportunity to send a message to our friends in Lublin that they could come and join us. Henry Szengut sent a special message to Cesia, and we all hoped that the way would now be clear for her to join us.

The first part of Finkel's mission was an unqualified success. In the hospital he enlisted the aid of two ghetto inmates, Dvoretzki and Berezyn, who were working in the storage room, my old hunting ground. Between the three of them, they succeeded in "organizing" a generous supply of things required for an effective fighting force, guns, ammunition, blankets and uniforms. They also commandeered a German army truck complete with an army driver to bring the goods to us. They told the German that he was not to ask any questions and that he would be paid well for his troubles. Along with the weapons, sixteen people from the prison camp, including Dvoretzki, were loaded into the truck.

When the truck arrived at a secluded place near our camp, Dvoretzki waved a pistol into the German driver's face. "We'll have to get off here," he said. "You go back where you came from and you'd better be quiet about what you saw and where you went today. If you talk, you'll be a goner, because if the Germans won't kill you, we'll get you some day."

Fate works in odd ways. Dvoretzki, a short, handsome, blond young man, had served in the Polish army until the fall of Poland. He was in Lipova 7 along with us. After the war, in Germany, he married and looked for a place where he and his young bride would be able to start upon a new life. But things did not turn out the way he expected. On a rainy afternoon, driving on one of Ger-

53

many's super-highways, the German driver of the car in which Dvoretzki and the Rubinsteins were passengers swerved to avoid a collision with another car. His own car left the highway and plunged down the embankment. The Rubinsteins were injured but survived. Dvoretzki was killed instantly.

However, all this was still part of the distant future when Finkel returned to our camp with the German loot and sixteen of our friends. Finkel had done his job well. Now there was for each one of us a German army rifle and a German uniform coat. Tolka, the Russian, pronounced us ready to fight the Germans.

But Finkel had not brought back Cesia Wrobel because Cesia was dead. She had been in the habit of taking off her armband with the Star of David that all Jews were required to wear. Armed with forged identification papers, she would leave the ghetto and mingle with the Poles to gossip and do a little business. She did not look Jewish, so she got away with it for some time. But one day she was caught and shot right then and there—not because she was Jewish but because of her false identification pass.

At first, Henry refused to believe it. He was stunned. So often they had been in the habit of imagining escaping to the forest together. He had lived in the hope that, some happy day when the war was over, he and Cesia would set out for a brighter future. Now it seemed to Henry that there was no point to living, no more promise of happiness for which it was worth fighting to survive. For some time I was afraid that Henry might take his own life, and I kept very close to him.

Not long before, we had lost another one of our group: Kaganovich. He had gone with Szengut, Tolka, and some of the Markuszow men to get weapons from the Poles. They were stopped by a German patrol. Szengut and Tolka were unharmed, but several of the others were killed. Among the dead was Kaganovich. The next morning we went into the forest to bury him. We took away with us his personal possessions, his gun, his wrist watch, his cigarette lighter and some gold coins. Poor Kaganovich no longer had any use for them, but we had no way of knowing when we, the living, might need these things to buy survival for ourselves in a hostile world.

We became part of a larger unit, the refugees from Markuszow. Later, we were to be joined by other Jews who had fled from their homes in nearby villages to escape the Nazis.

XI

Drop's Farm

The winter of 1942-43 was exceptionally harsh. The snow was very deep. This hampered us in making our usual rounds for food because we feared that our footprints in the snow might give us away to the Germans. Worse, the peasants in the area became increasingly hostile. Most of them were wealthy but did not take kindly to the idea that they should be called upon to feed Jews. More often than not, our men approaching a farmhouse would be met by ferocious dogs. Some of the peasants organized themselves into a self-defense force to keep the Jewish partisans away. In one village the peasants set the church bell ringing to alert the Germans. Soon we were losing people almost every day; the Poles were turning them over to the German authorities. Eventually, instead of fighting the Germans, we were forced to fight Poles who made common cause with the Nazis when it came to killing Jews.

We had to make a stand somewhere, or else we would all be destroyed. One night two of our men, Morel and Shmuel Topper carrying his precious machine gun, led a small group on a food-gathering mission to a village where we had always been given a friendly reception. But this time our comrades suddenly found themselves surrounded by Poles and a pack of vicious, snarling dogs. Before they could regain their wits, Morel and Shmuel had

55

their machine gun taken from them and found themselves forced against a wall. The Poles opened fire on them. The others in the group escaped, but Morel and Shmuel were killed.

The news sent our whole camp into an uproar. We decided to take drastic action. Jaeger and I led a patrol of 20 men, including a band of Markuszow boys under Sever Rubinstein, to the village. We ordered all the villagers out of their houses and herded them together into the village square. There, we told them how we felt about Poles who, instead of fighting the Nazis, attacked their own countrymen for no other reason but that they were Jews. We were going to make an object lesson of their village, as a warning to other Poles who might feel tempted to follow their example. We advised them to get away as far as possible from their village if they did not want to die. They got the idea at once, and fled as fast as their legs could carry them. After we had cleared the village of its entire population, including horses, cows and birds, we set fire to the barns and houses. Within hours, the village had been reduced to a pile of rubble. On the way back to our camp, we scattered some crudely lettered leaflets on the road, telling what we had done to that particular village, and why. But not all the Poles we met were evil. Back in the Garbow district there was a farmer named Drop who became a special friend. His family consisted of his wife and his aged father. Drop did not dare let us into his house, for fear of what the Germans might do to the woman and the old man if we were caught there. However, he had a stable where he kept his horses. Just behind that stable was a small chamber with stone walls and a trap door which led down into a large, warm cellar. Drop said that we could make the cellar our headquarters until we were ready to move on. Every day Drop's wife would come to us from the house carrying trays loaded with food. To shield the food from prying eyes outside, she covered it with a variety of strange objects. One day she staggered into our cellar with a huge leather saddle which she put down very gently and then removed from the floor to reveal a roast chicken.

Drop hated the Germans and was genuinely fond of us. His father liked to reminisce about the days when his home town had been under the rule of the Russian Tsars. He said that the Tsars and the Greek Orthodox priests were to blame for the Jew-hatred of the peasants. The peasants had been a superstitious lot and believed anything the priests told them. As a result, it had been an easy thing for the priests and the Tsarist police to teach them that the Jews were not only Christ-killers but also dangerous revolutionaries. The peasants in the village where the elder Drop had been born had hardly ever seen a Jew at close range, but they firmly believed the hoary myth that each year at Passover the Jews killed Christian children and drank their blood as a sacrifice to their deity. After the fall of the Tsarist empire and the founding of the Polish republic, the old man said, emotions had quieted down somewhat, but now the Germans were stirring things up all over again by preaching to the peasants that all the Jews were Bolsheviks out to cheat the poor peasants of their hard-earned possessions.

But if the Drops hated the Germans, there was one person whom they hated even more and that was the Soltys, the district leader. This was awkward for us because the Soltys happened to be close to our other friend, Genek Kaminsky, the underground chief. But we could not afford to antagonize Drop, and so when Drop suggested that we raid the Soltys' farm and steal some of his ducks and chickens, we had no other choice but to oblige him. After all, Drop was our best friend.

After several weeks at the Drop farm, we left to rejoin our friends, the Markuszow group. While we had been away, they had been joined by a group of Jews from the town of Kurov, and a number of young men who called themselves "the Cossacks." Actually, these youths were Jews from Markuszow, but they did not look Jewish and did not want it known that they were anything but pure-bred Poles. They all wore Polish army uniforms which they had bought from Polish soldiers and they seemed to be forever on the move. They were full of fighting spirit but totally undisciplined, and sometimes Jaeger, Sever Rubinstein and I felt that it would be better for all of us if they were not such good marksmen but would learn to obey orders.

To hear the "Cossacks" talk, their prime objective was not to fight the Germans but to seek out girls. Instead of making their forays at night and lying low during the daytime, they walked about in broad daylight and got drunk together with the peasants. This may have been quite a natural thing for high-spirited young boys, but it put our group and the Markuszow unit into dire peril.

I felt that if only they could be put in their place, they would make a valuable asset, for they were certainly courageous. One night I took them along with some of my own men on a food foraging expedition. They started off with us, but when we approached the village that had been our target for the night, our trouble began. There was an air of unusual silence about the village that night. As a rule, the mere approach of a stranger would set all the dogs barking, but this time we heard not a sound. It occurred to me that the peasants might have set a trap for us and I told the men that we had better move on to another village. My own men and I turned back, but the "Cossacks" would not hear of giving up. They knew the peasants in this village, they said, and would have less trouble getting food from them than we would. They were quite friendly with a number of girls from the farms. I felt my blood pressure rise, but there was no use arguing with such hotheads. And so my men and I went away, leaving the "Cossacks" to their luck.

We had not gone far when we heard the sound of gunfire from the direction of the village. We ran back, on the double. It was as I had suspected. It had been a German trap. Later, we learned the whole story. One of the peasants had alerted the Germans, who had been waiting to pounce upon the intruders. The Germans herded the "Cossacks" into the village square and killed all but two of them, Jusiek and Marcinek. Jusiek, a hard-as-nails type from a village near Lublin, was to lose his life later on. Marcinek was to survive the war. Handsome, suave and skilled in the art of making friends, he eventually settled in France.

After this incident, I considered that it was time for us to move on. We had heard reports that a large partisan unit had become active on the German banks of the River Bug, the natural boundary between the German and Russian sectors of Poland. Most of these partisans were Russian soldiers who had escaped from nearby German POW camps. An impressive number of them, we were told, happened to be Jews. It seemed to me that we should join them, if for no other reason but to get into some real action against the Germans. We had frittered away our energies fighting Polish peasants and a German patrol here and there. I, for one, was eager to do a little more.

Jaeger, Tolka and I called a brief meeting. It was agreed that a small group, consisting of my own men, should try to make contact with the Russian partisans and then send word to the others whether or not the rest should also follow. Among the men who volunteered to go with me were Szengut, Stefan Finkel, Zelazny Eisenberg, Andreiev, and the boy from Maidanek who, in the meantime, had completely recovered from his illness and appeared to be as fit as any of us others, perhaps even a little more so. "Maidanek," as we had come to call him because no one seemed to know his real name, was fired by a sense of mission. He was convinced that there was some great task waiting to be fulfilled by him—else, why should he have been permitted to escape death twice—first from the very threshold of the Maidanek gas chambers and then from the ravages of typhus?

XII

Encounter with German Troops

It was late December, 1942, when we set out on our journey east toward the River Bug. Our first big hurdle on the way was the River Wieprz, some 50 kilometers west of the Bug. We were to cross the Wieprz at a point in the south. But unfortunately the bridge which crossed the Wieprz at the south was the main railroad supply line linking the cities of Warsaw and Lublin; naturally, we could expect the bridge to be heavily guarded by German troops.

We reached the river at night. The deep snow bathed the landscape in an eerie moonlike light. The railroad bridge was far down the river, but it was clearly visible, for it was brilliantly illuminated by great spotlights. I was surprised that the Germans would permit this, for it seemed to make the bridge a sitting target for enemy aircraft. But then perhaps the Germans reasoned that the nearest Russian air base was too far away to make a raid on the bridge worthwhile for the Soviets.

It was obvious that there would be no way for us to get across the river unseen. To use the bridge was, of course, out of the question, nor would it be possible to wade through this river as we had through the creek on the outskirts of Lublin; the Wieprz was much to wide and deep for that.

We had to keep moving, and so we marched northward along

the banks of the river. I was cold and depressed. Had I done the right thing to bring my men here? It seemed a waste of precious time and provisions. By dawn we came upon a cluster of farmsteads nestled close to the river's edge. Some men were signalling and calling to a boat in the river which was moving toward shore. The boat was small, and I judged that it would take three journeys to get us all across, but I was ready to chance it. When the boat landed and its passengers had gone ashore, I stopped the boatsman, a wizened old Pole, and asked him whether he would be willing to ferry us across the river. We would be glad to pay him whatever he charged, we said. The men on the shore looked at us with some suspicion, but a few banknotes were sufficient persuasion for the old boatsman.

Arriving safely on the east bank of the river, we made for the woods. I lagged behind, stopping frequently to carve notches with my knife into the barks of trees so that we would be able to find our way back to the river in a hurry, if need be. We were now on unknown territory, and had no idea what kind of people might be living in these parts. We stopped a peasant and asked him the way to the nearest farm, but he only shrugged his shoulders and went on quickly. I have no doubt that after the arduous trek from our camp we looked pretty wild, and I could not blame the man for wanting to avoid trouble.

We hid out in the forest until nightfall, and then resumed our march. By dawn the next morning, we came to a farmhouse and headed for its gate. A woman rushed out waving her arms excitedly.

"Please don't come in!" she shouted. "I have a sick child inside. She has diphtheria."

But we were dog-tired and in no mood to go on.

"There's no need to upset yourself, Miss," I reassured her. "We won't go into your house, and we won't bother you. We'll just go into your barn to rest for a little while."

The woman seemed to have no objections and we promptly made for the barn, closing the double door behind us. Within moments, we all were asleep on the floor. As we usually did in such cases, we picked one of our men to do guard duty and alert us in case of trouble, but as it turned out, the poor fellow was unable to keep himself awake, much to our misfortune.

61

When I awoke, all the others were still asleep. I saw a crack of light on the wall; it was pale gray. What time was it? Still daybreak? Of course not. It was late afternoon; the winter days were short and the light faded rapidly. We had slept all day long. I crept toward the barn door and opened it just enough to be able to peer out with one eye. I saw the path which we had used the day before. Then, it had been smoothly blanketed in white by the steadily falling snow; now, it was streaked with muddy brown cart tracks. I could hear voices, and they were coming closer. It was men, and they were speaking in German.

I swore softly to myself. So the woman had tipped off the Germans! I closed the door and awakened my men by putting my hand over the mouth of each one in turn to muffle the sounds of rude awakening. Then, my knapsack on my back and my gun at the ready, I went back to the door. Now I could see them moving toward the back of the barn, German soldiers, accompanied by Polish policemen. I signaled to my men. They grabbed their rifles and, with a loud war whoop, poured out of the barn, firing right and left and scattering our attackers. The maneuver had worked; we had caught the Germans off balance. Some of the Germans had been hit and were lying on the ground. But I did not stop and look. By the time the Germans had regained their wits and begun to fire at us, we were well ahead of them, fanning out, running zigzag and leaping like stags over the snowdrifts. I felt a sudden sting in my little finger and realized that I had been hit. I cried out and put my finger into my mouth. Henry Szengut was running next to me, crouching low.

Straight ahead, I saw one of our men go down, hit in the back and knee. Two more men fell at my right; one of them was "Maidanek." So his fantastic luck had run out after all. And then I felt a searing pain in my left calf and fell to the ground. I struggled up, lurched forward but fell again. Henry Szengut dragged me to my feet but I kept sinking into the snow. Blood was streaming from my leg. But fear proved stronger than weakness or pain and, with Szengut holding me up, we ran a three-legged race, hopping over the snowdrifts. We had to keep going because the Germans were upon our heels. The only weapons Szengut and I now had between us were my rifle, one hand grenade and one pistol. Szengut said that if we were going to be captured by the Germans

62

we should rather use the hand grenade to kill ourselves first. My instinct dictated me rather to choose life.

I shouted to our comrades ahead of us; they stopped, turned around and opened fire on the Germans in the rear. Caught off balance once again, the Germans threw themselves flat on the ground. They no longer ran so fast after that.

Meanwhile, Szengut and I were able to move on some distance onto a highway and from there to a forest. Eventually, the others joined us there. We made our roll call. Except for the three men whom I had seen fall, no one else in our party was missing. Szengut and Finkel still hoped that "Maidanek" and the two others had only been wounded and had managed to get to safety. I was not so optimistic; I felt certain that all three had died. Poor "Maidanek," death had caught up with him before he could perform the mission he had felt so sure was his foreordained task.

Only now did I notice that Szengut, without whom I would surely have collapsed and probably died, had also been wounded; he had been hit in the palm of his left hand.

By now my own finger had begun to hurt, and my leg was bleeding badly. I tore a piece of cloth from my undershirt and tied it around my leg. My finger was bleeding, too, but I did not pay attention to that.

By nightfall, I could no longer move my leg. While Szengut and I wondered what to do, a horse and wagon passed. The driver was an elderly man, wrapped in a thick fur coat. Szengut and Finkel stopped the wagon. I told the man that I had been wounded in the leg. At first, he did not seem to understand, but when he saw the blood stains on my pants leg, he offered to take me to his house for first aid.

Szengut and Finkel helped me onto the wagon. They asked the man where he lived, then disappeared. About fifteen minutes later I heard a loud explosion. The driver of the wagon and I turned to see where the noise could have come from, but the thick trees screened everything from view except the snow-covered highway straight ahead.

As we reached the edge of the forest, there were Szengut and Finkel, running towards us, shouting and waving their arms. The driver pulled his horse's reins and the wagon came to an abrupt stop. "We've just blown up the forest ranger's house!" Finkel yelled. Without troubling themselves to ask the driver's permission, the two men jumped onto the wagon and told their story. They had gone to the house of the local forest ranger on a hunch that "Maidanek" and the two other missing men had found shelter there. The door was not locked, and when they entered the house they found there not our three missing comrades but at least a dozen German soldiers seated around a table, drinking beer and lustily bawling Nazi party songs. They were too drunk, apparently, to notice that two strangers had entered the hall. Szengut and Finkel turned around, went out and softly closed the door behind them. Once outside, Szengut took out the hand grenade with which he had wanted to blow up the two of us when things had seemed so utterly hopeless for us, and hurled it through the window into the house. Then he and Finkel ran off as fast as their legs could carry them. That, then, was the explosion I had heard. Quite a few German soldiers must have died for their fatherland inside that Polish forest ranger's house.

XIII

We Lose Szengut

The driver of the wagon informed us that he would not be able to bring the three of us into his house without first alerting his wife and children that they were about to have some visitors. "The wife hasn't been too well, lately, you know," he explained. "She's a little nervous about sudden visitors." He told us that he owned a large farm, and that he would take us to the house of his manager until he could prepare his wife and children for our coming. To me, it seemed odd that he wanted to have us anywhere near his farm. People who went around blowing up forest rangers' houses were not exactly fit company for nervous women.

We turned off into a narrow path and came upon a long, low building, actually, two cottages, one two floors high, the other just one, joined together at an angle. A man in the courtyard was forking up small bits of hay onto a four-wheeled barrow. The farmer climbed down from his wagon and exchanged a few words with the man. To my surprise, I noticed a familiar face; Piasecki, another man from our advance party, had also found his way to the farm. He, too, had been looking for "Maidanek" and the two other men whom we had lost in the skirmish with the Germans. Piasecki helped me down from the wagon. I was in great pain. The woman of the house came out; she first looked at Szengut's hand, then turned to me. The farmer, meanwhile, had driven off in his wagon at a fast trot. I wanted very badly to lie down and rest my leg. The woman and her husband both seemed pleasant people. They helped me into the house with Szengut following. After giving us some hot soup, the woman helped me upstairs to the second floor and led me into a room directly above the kitchen. There was a cot in the room. "Lie down here," she said.

The room was large, with a small window that looked upon the front garden. In the floor, at one end of the room, which ran the length of the building, there was an open trap door, revealing the top of a ladder.

Szengut made a careful inspection of the layout while the woman was attending to my leg. She carefully cleansed the wound with disinfectant, then packed it with cotton. "You leave that cotton in the wound," she explained. "It'll absorb all the pus." She really seemed knowledgeable and I considered myself lucky to get such efficient care.

"Here's some powder to help you sleep. You could use a good. couple of hours' rest," the woman said. I did not like the idea of taking medicine I did not know, but I knew that I needed a few hours free of the intense, throbbing pain that had all but paralyzed my left leg.

Piasecki came to check up on me. "Don't worry about sleeping," he reassured me. "I'll stay up and watch over things." Szengut disappeared into the next room, then returned to tell me that ten other men from our advance party had arrived and set up camp outside. I lay back on my cot. Before I knew it, the powder was doing its work and I was fast asleep.

We rested at the farmhouse most of the day. By the time we had recovered our senses somewhat, we began to wonder why we had had no word from the farmer. How long could it take him to prepare his wife and children for our arrival?

"Don't worry," the man said, "you can stay at my house as long as you like. You're safe here."

When night came, the rest of the men also moved into the house and were assigned places to sleep. I shared my room with Szengut, Piasecki and a third man, Matros.

Before dawn the next morning, the woman of the house appeared, wished us a cheerful good morning and brought us some eggs, bread and cheese. I ate my breakfast with gusto. I felt rested and my leg did not seem to hurt quite so badly as it had the day before.

Suddenly, Matros, who had gone out of the room a few minutes before, burst into the room, hissed: "German soldiers!" and darted out again. Then Szengut rushed to the little window and looked out. "They're all over the courtyard!" he yelled and raced outside. I could hear him leaping down the few steps to the adjoining house. Next, I heard windows being flung open, gunfire outside, the tramp of heavy boots on the floor below, and more gunfire.

Piasecki was standing at the other end of the room, bending over the open trap door, talking to someone at the foot of the steps and at the same time gesticulating frantically at me. I hobbled over to the trap door. The ladder of which I had seen the top emerging from the trap door led down into darkness. In the shadows at the bottom stood the man of the house.

I called to Szengut, but there was no answer. I limped to the door and called again. Still no sign of Szengut. I heard the sound of footsteps on the floors and the rattling of window panes. Piasecki pulled me to the trap door:

"Let's go! There's no time to lose! Szengut'll be all right! Let's get moving."

Piasecki almost dragged me down the ladder. At the bottom, I found myself face to face with my host, his pale features lit from the trap door above. We were in a passage of some sort. Together he and Piasecki pulled me along until we came to a narrow door, which the farmer opened up gently. We found ourselves in a small courtyard surrounded by a high wall, lined with rabbit hutches and chicken coops.

Piasecki and the farmer pushed me to the top of the wall and told me to let myself drop over the side. They followed close behind. We fell onto a snow-covered compost heap. Around us was an orchard of bare trees, laden here and there with white balls of snow. The sky above was a pale gray. The sun had not yet risen.

I kept looking back anxiously, watching for a sign of the other men and Szengut. The farm manager said that they had escaped on the other side of the building and would be making straight for the woods from there. "You go through this orchard," he instructed us, "and head for the woods from this side. Eventually, you'll meet the others. Now go! Go!" he shouted. Then he turned around, leaving Piasecki and me on our own.

Piasecki piloted me along the trees at a fairly quick pace. The shooting had apparently stopped. We had already passed the orchard and were crossing a narrow piece of land toward the woods.

As we hobbled along, I said to Piasecki that the farmer who had brought us to his house in his wagon was probably to blame for our plight. In all likelihood he had thought that we were bandits, terrorizing the countryside. Perhaps the forest ranger whose house Finkel and Szengut had blown up had been his friend, and he had felt it only proper to report us to the German authorities. Piasecki was angry at me for even suggesting that the farmer might have given us away to the Germans. After all, the Germans were just as much the farmer's enemies as they were ours, he insisted. I said I only hoped the farmer knew this, too. I was still certain that, in this thickly wooded region, the Gemans could not possibly have found us without some help.

We walked all day and night, with only brief stops for rest. On the whole, my leg did not give me too much trouble. Whatever the truth had been about the manager, he and his wife had certainly taken good care of my wound.

Just before dawn we emerged from the woods and came upon a Polish farm boy. The surroundings seemed strangely familiar. I could not believe my eyes. We were back at the farm from which we had fled. We had passed through the forest circle-fashion, coming out again precisely at the place where we had entered the woods.

"Say, what are you doing here?" the boy demanded. "The Germans are after you. They were here and killed one of your men right inside the house. I saw them take the body away in a wagon."

I was seized by a terrible premonition. Could it have been Szengut?

"The dead man, what did he look like?" I asked.

The boy was too excited to listen. "You know," he continued, "the farmer was there, too. He came with the Germans."

So I had been right after all!

"Come on, boy," I persisted. "Try to remember! The dead man, did you see him? What did he look like? Tall? Short?"

"I dunno, Mister. They had him wrapped in a blanket. But you shouldn't be here. They all left, these Germans. But they'll be back, with lots more soldiers. And they'll be searching the woods. And the man and the woman in this house, the Germans tied them up and took them away, too."

So our hosts had had to pay dearly for their decency. Their own employer, the rich old farmer with the wagon and the fur coat, had given them away to the Germans, who probably made short order of them.

A woman, carrying a basket filled with eggs, appeared.

"That's my mother," the boy said.

When the woman saw us, she became quite excited and told us to follow her. She led us into a cottage hidden behind the trees and gave us some bread and cheese. I got out my map, the old map from Lublin, and started making plans where to go next. Piasecki and I felt that we should go back to the River Wieprz; this, I said, would be our only chance of finding the rest of our men again.

We thanked the boy and his mother, and set out once more. It was a long, dreary trek through the snowy forest, and I was becoming increasingly tired. My leg, which had seemed a little better before, had become so swollen that I felt it only as a numb, dead weight.

After a whole night of marching, we arrived at the banks of the Wieprz. The place was deserted. We dropped to the ground for a few hours of sleep. By the time we awoke it was late afternoon. We wandered along the river's edge for some distance.

The river was winding. Coming around a bend, we could hear the drone of trucks. It turned out that, about 500 paces from us, there was a highway, which had been screened from our view by a curtain of fir trees. We sat down to study my map and from the shape of the river and the proximity of the highway tried to pinpoint our position.

69

Just then we heard children shouting. A group of school boys came running out from among the trees. When they saw us, they began to yell, *"Zhyd! Zhyd!* ("Jew-boys! Jew-boys!)"

I looked to my right and my left, and said a silent prayer that no one should have heard them. Unlike the river bank, the highway was anything but deserted.

The order of the day was to shake the boys and move on. Keep cool and calm, I told myself. It'll do the trick. So I got up, laughed, and said to them in an ordinary voice, as if nothing could have been more obvious:

"Sure we're Jew-boys! Haven't you ever seen Jewish people before? What's the big idea of all that racket? Don't you know the highways are full of Nazis? Do you want them to find us here? They're the enemies of Poland, they want to make slaves out of all of us. You, your parents, everybody."

I stopped for a moment, then changed my voice from kindliness to anger.

"Or maybe that's just what you would want, to bring the Germans here. Maybe you're just yellow. Maybe you are enemies of Poland yourselves?"

I had made my point...The boys stood still for a moment, looking at each other. One of them asked where we had come from and where we were going.

"We want to cross the river," I said. "We need a man who'll row us across. But if you keep on making such a racket we'll have to run away back into the woods or else the Germans'll be on top of us and we'll have to fight them...And then where will you be?"

At that moment a tall man in a leather jacket and fur cap came into view. One of the boys whispered his name and they all ran off. Evidently, this was an important character. It occurred to me that he might be the schoolmaster.

The man seemed friendly enough. After the boys had vanished, he pointed with his cane to my leg.

"Are you in trouble?"

"Yes. I got hit. By the Germans."

He quickly glanced about him, his eyes wide with alarm.

"When did this happen? Where?"

I told him, and he seemed relieved that it had been a few days before and some distance away. I explained that we now wanted to cross the river.

"Follow me," he said. "I know a boatsman around here."

He strode along the river bank without saying anything more. A few hundred paces further on, a side stream flowed into the Wieprz, and at that point there was a low wooden shed which turned out to be a boathouse. Our escort called out something, and presently a white-bearded old man, wearing a fur hat, emerged. It was hard for us to understand what the old man was saying. His long mustache all but covered his mouth, and he seemed to be chewing on some food. Also, he spoke in a strange Polish dialect. The gist of the conversation was that he wanted money, lots of money. I had no money on me, but I still had in my knapsack the wrist watch and the cigarette lighter which I had taken from the body of our comrade Kaganovich.

I produced the lighter, held it out to the boatsman, and made the lighter work. As the little flame popped up, a gleam came into the boatsman's eyes and he nodded quickly.

"Come," he said.

There must have been a wooden bridge nearby, for I could hear a truck rolling over it, rattling the planks as if they were loose. The tall man in the leather jacket heard it, too, and bade us a hurried good-bye, making off in the other direction at a fast pace.

Piasecki and I climbed into the boat. As the old man rowed us across, I thought of poor Kaganovich. He was gone, but his cigarette lighter had helped save us.

After we had landed on the other side of the river, we hurried off into the forest. This was no longer strange territory. We made for the village of Staroschin, because we knew that this was on the way to the farm of our old friend Drop.

As we approached the village, Piasecki told me to sit down and rest, while he went ahead to find a farmhouse where we might get some food, and perhaps even shelter for the night.

About half an hour later he returned, quite excited. I struggled to my feet and hobbled toward him, in the direction he indicated. There was a farmhouse with a light in the window, and I followed Piasecki inside.

As I stood in the door, I heard a great shout. There, before my eyes, crowding the little room, were the rest of my men. There were more shouts, and embraces. They had given me up for dead.

I looked into the faces of my comrades. There was one still missing.

"Where's Szengut?" I asked.

No one replied. Now I knew for certain. The man who had been killed in the farmhouse had been my friend, Henry Szengut.

I burst into tears. Szengut had been my best friend. Cultured, sensitive and gifted, he had trained to become an architect, but the war had interrupted his studies. For all too short a time he had found happiness with Cesia. I know that he had lived in the hope that, when the war was over, he would be able to return to his profession and that they would set up a home together. With Cesia's death, life seemed to have lost all meaning for Henry. Still he had kept doggedly on: although all joy had vanished from his personal life, he had felt it his duty to lend every ounce of energy to the common bid for freedom. Both of us had memories of Cesia and, with her death, we were no longer rivals. In our grief, we had come together more than ever. He remained a faithful friend until the last, and had saved my life after I had been wounded by the Germans. I, on the other hand, had run away from the farmhouse with Piasecki without waiting for him. Had I borne him some kind of subconscious grudge for taking my girl? I could never forgive myself for abandoning him. My grief was mixed with a sense of guilt.

The other men seemed to guess my thoughts. "Pull yourself together! There's nothing you could have done," said Stefan Finkel gruffly. "They only would have killed you too. With your leg, you wouldn't have stood a chance." I had to accept this interpretation of events, which was only common sense in order to go on at all. I even felt envious of Henry and Cesia. My two best friends had been lovers for a short time, and now both were dead. They had taken the easy way out. Without them, the path that opened out before me was a lonely and an uninviting one.

XIV

On the Move

We spent the night at the farmhouse. Early the next morning we set out for the Garbow forest, there were altogether nine of us. We had heard that Jaeger, Tolka and some of Tolka's friends from the Markuszow group were building a bunker out in the woods, and we wanted to find them.

After a few hours' march my leg began to give me trouble again. I told the others to go scouting for some food and leave me to rest for a few hours. We agreed upon a time when, if all was well, they would return for me. Matros insisted on staying behind with me. He was a pleasant, gentle fellow, perhaps almost too gentle for a partisan fighter. But he was to survive the war and to make a new life for himself in Israel.

Matros and I waited the entire day for the others to return. By nightfall I was sure that they had been captured by the Germans. Finally, Matros and I decided to start out for the woods on our own.

It took us all night to get to the forest. At dawn we came upon the bunker where we found an older man, and a young girl. They turned out to be the father and sister of Sever Rubinstein from the Markuszow group.

"What's going on?" I demanded. "Where's Tolka?"

"Tolka took off," Rubinstein's father replied. "He was afraid the Germans knew about our bunker. So he went further into the woods to build another bunker for us."

While we were talking, Tolka, accompanied by Jaeger, suddenly appeared. And before long, much to our relief, the seven men who had set out with me from the farmhouse the previous morning turned up alone. I asked Tolka to put us up in his new bunker, at least for one day. But Tolka replied that this was out of the question: the bunker could not possibly hold all of us.

"But you can take this man, can't you?" the young girl demanded, waving her hand in my direction. "Can't you see he's wounded? He needs a place to rest."

Tolka seemed ill at ease. "Look, Blimka," he said to the girl. "We don't have room for any new people. He can't stay there, and that's that." Perhaps he did not want anyone outside his immediate entourage to know about the new bunker, much less to see it.

The nine of us put our heads together. We were on our own. What were we to do? We agreed that we did not have another alternative but to go to the house of our old friend, the farmer Drop. He would not turn us away.

Drop did not disappoint us. He bade us a hearty welcome and said we could stay in his cellar as long as we wished. He immediately inquired about Henry Szengut. When we told him what had happened to Henry, Drop cried. He had taken a real liking to Szengut. "What an end for such a decent young man," he lamented again and again.

Awkwardly for us, however, his grief for Szengut had not altered Drop's old house rule; whoever was Drop's friend had to hate the district leader, who unfortunately was a friend of our underground friend Genek Kaminsky. "I told you that you're free to stay in my cellar as long as you like, but there's one condition," Drop said. "You have to raid the Soltys' house and loot it, just as you did the last time you were here."

Drop's request placed us into an embarrassing position, to say the least. When we had raided the district leader's house before, we had been able to make a getaway without being discovered. But we could hardly expect such good fortune twice. If we were caught, we would be in trouble with Genek Kaminsky, whom we could ill afford to antagonize. On the other hand, we could not at this point risk being thrown out by Drop, whose hatred for the Soltys verged on obsession. So we decided to take our chances and go directly to the Soltys. But we performed our "raid" in an open, above-board manner. We paid him a polite visit, explaining that we were partisans fighting the enemies of Poland, and that we could do with some food. A few chickens, we said, would do very nicely. Luckily, the Soltys was sympathetic. He gave us the birds and we took them back in triumph to Drop, who was delighted that we had once again succeeded in robbing his long-time enemy.

During this period I would not have made a particularly good raider because my wounds were not healing properly. My leg still gave me considerable pain, but the worst trouble came from my finger, to which I had not given much attention in the beginning. It had become infected and had swollen to twice its size. I kept soaking it in boric acid supplied by Mrs. Drop but eventually my whole right hand became swollen and discolored. With today's antibiotics infections of this sort hardly ever progress to this stage, but at the time I had good reason to fear that I might get gangrene. Under the circumstances this would probably have meant the loss of my whole hand, if not of my life. Fortunately I had a good constitution, which, as doctors told me in America years later, helped me overcome the infection without drastic treatment. However, my finger has remained stiff to this day.

It may be that in the end my finger and leg really healed because, probably for the first time in my life, I had five or six weeks of complete rest. That winter of 1942-43 was very severe and snow fell without a stop so that we were, in effect, snowbound. It was a good thing that we had our hideout in Drop's warm cellar. From time to time one or two of our men would go out in search of food, and return with news of our other comrades, It turned out that Tolka's bunker was not as small as Tolka wanted us to believe. Forty or fifty of our comrades were now hiding out there. Sever Rubinstein's father, however, had not moved into Tolka's new bunker; he was staying on the farm of an elderly woman who had come to Poland from France many years before and who was also sheltering several other Jews from Lublin. Rubinstein's son David, his wife Bella, and David's sister Blimka had found quarters at other farmhouses nearby. Sever was with Tolka.

However, as the month of January, 1943, drew to a close we realized that we would soon have to leave Drop's farm because the area was no longer safe for us. One day a Jewish boy who had escaped from a labor camp not far away ran through Drop's field with some German soldiers in hot pursuit. Drop saw the boy vanish into the woods. In order to divert the Germans, Drop invited them into his home and plied them with food and drinks. Meanwhile, Mrs. Drop came to us in the cellar and warned us to lie low until the Germans would leave. We immediately readied our rifles for action to defend not only ourselves but also the Drops. We knew that if the Germans found out that Drop and his wife were giving shelter to Jewish partisans, they would kill the Drops and burn down the farmstead. This was the customary procedure the Germans followed whenever they caught a Polish peasant hiding underground fighters. But Mrs. Drop did not appear unduly concerned. "Never mind your guns," she said calmly. "My husband knows how to deal with Germans."

Drop kept the Germans eating, drinking and joking long enough to enable the boy to flee well out of their reach. Hours later the Germans, heavy with good food, left the farm. Apparently they had called off the hunt, because Drop had heard one of them say to the others, "We might as well let the Jew boy go to the devil. He won't live long in that forest. Too much snow. He won't make it. None of them ever do."

Then, one day early in February, 1943, Drop himself came into our cellar hideout. For the first time, we saw him worried and upset. "I've got bad news, men," he said. "The Germans got Tolka. Some farmer must have tipped the Germans off, and they blew up the bunker. Tolka is dead and so is everybody else. Nobody was left alive."

The news came like a thunderbolt. Forty of our comrades including Jaeger, dead! As for Drop, the report had made him lose his nerve. He explained that he did not want to turn us out of his home, but that he was afraid to keep us any longer. Clearly the Germans were searching the area. What if they caught him with a cellar full of Jewish partisan fighters? We made it easier for him: we told him that we ourselves did not think it safe for us to stay with him any longer. His neighbors might find out that he had been hiding us at his farm and report him to the Germans.

76

And so, on February 9, 1943, a bright, clear, winter day, we left Drop's farm and plodded through the snow to the nearby village of Pryzcowa-Gura. There we knew several peasants who had, in fact, given us shelter on other occasions. We were in luck, for this time, too, they readily took us in for the night. The next morning we proceeded to the forest on the other side of the village. Much to our surprise we came upon a group of men marching in the direction of Pryzcowa-Gura. When they shouted out the password, *"Amcha!"* we realized, to our incredulous relief, that at least one group of Tolka's men had survived the German raid on the bunker. We eagerly questioned them and learned that quite a few more inmates of the ill-fated bunker were still alive, among them Jaeger and Sever Rubinstein. They had been seen moving about in the forest; they could not be far away. Before long we actually found them, well equipped with weapons and wearing warm winter greatcoats. After a boisterous exchange of greetings, Jaeger explained to us how he and 14 others had escaped being blown to bits by the Germans: Tolka had sent them out to forage for food so that they had been away from the bunker at the time of the explosion.

We all agreed that we had been far too passive all winter long. The time had come for us to emerge from hiding and to begin harassing the Germans. Several hours later we found in the forest another group of partisans, Jews from the town of Kalmionka, near Lubartow. They were led by Franek Blaichman, who was nicknamed "Skinny" because he was so painfully thin. He was then only a lad of 20, but he knew how to cope with the dangers and hardships of partisan life.

We suggested to Blaichman and his men that they should join forces with our group. Together, we organized into a larger unit which we called the Emilia Plater Unit after the Polish Joan of Arc who had fought valiantly in the Polish war of liberation during the 19th century.

We next sought out our Polish underground friend, Genek Kaminsky, to have him suggest a plan of action against the Germans, and also to hear what was going on in the world—for we knew that Genek had a radio. Genek told us the latest news from the Eastern front, and from North Africa, where British and American forces were giving the Germans a bad time. Kaminsky

The Emilia Plater group in the Garbow woods (1943).

made it plain that there was plenty of work for us to do. He mentioned that large bodies of Russian troops which had been cut off on the German side of the River Bug had taken to the woods and were fighting the Germans guerrilla-fashion. He also suggested that we try to join a larger unit of partisans, under the command of a man called Chil, an underground fighter well known for his daring. Chil's group, which was on the other side of the River Wieprz, was receiving weapons and ammunition dropped from Russian planes. The partisan units, Kaminsky complained, were not as well organized as a coordinated fighting force should be. He felt that we should set up a proper intelligence network; once that was done, the Russians would drop not only small weapons but also radio transmitters and explosives for large-scale sabotage operations. Once we had the proper tools, we could blow up bridges, highways and railroad tracks of which there were quite a number in our area. In this manner we would be able to hurt the enemy by disrupting his communication lines.

But even before that, Kaminsky said, there was a job for us to do in the immediate neighborhood. The Germans had occupied a farm nearby, had done away with the farmer and were using the farm as a base for raids on partisans and other Poles. Kaminsky instructed us to mount a surprise attack on the Germans and drive them from the farm; however, we were to avoid killing them because the German authorities might then retaliate by exterminating the entire village. Our aim should be simply to liberate the farm and divest the Germans of their weapons, particularly machine guns.

We set out that night, a full party of 20 men, dispersing and keeping contact by sound signals. We took up positions and by dawn the next morning had closed in on the farm. We overpowered a German sentry, grabbed his rifle, then ordered him to go into the house and tell his friends that the place was surrounded. If they did not come out reaching for the sky, they would all be blown to pieces.

The German did as he was told, and he soon returned, followed by a few Germans with their arms in the air. Jusiek, who had narrowly escaped from a German trap earlier in the winter jumped the first German and was clearly elated with his success. But then the front door of the house burst open, and out rushed a German sergeant, roaring like a bull, his machine gun blazing away, firing in every direction. His aim was so wild that he even hit one of his own men, but unfortunately he also hit Jusiek in the arm. Jusiek fell to the ground, screaming in pain and terror.

Luckily the sergeant's gun jammed at this point. Some of our men then attacked him from behind with their rifle butts, while others picked up Jusiek and quickly carried him away. More shouts came from inside the building; it sounded as if we had stirred up a whole platoon of Germans. There was nothing to do but to make a retreat. The results of this, our first raiding operation, had been something less than successful, but at least we had not lost any men and we still had in our possession the rifle taken from the German sentry. Every rifle counted.

We took Jusiek to a nearby farm and asked the farmer to give him first aid. The farmer cleansed Jusiek's wound and bandaged it. Much to our relief, it turned out to be only a flesh wound; the bullet had not touched nerve or bone.

Our next operation, about a month later, was our first attempt at sabotage, and this time we did not do too badly. Our target was a railroad track on the line that linked the cities of Lublin and Warsaw. Since we had no explosives, our idea was to derail a train simply by pulling up the tracks at a certain spot.

It is not so easy to pull up a railroad track with tools one might ordinarily expect to find only on a farm or in a workshop, but we did the trick. Then we hid behind some bushes and watched the first train come along. It was a very long freight train. As we learned later, it carried no ammunition and almost no passengers, but the "accident" interrupted railroad traffic almost for an entire day.

XV

Enemies - Germans and Poles

A few days later a group of our men went back to the village of Pryzcowa-Gura, where we spent the night at the house of a peasant we knew. The next morning, however, the peasant said to us:

"Look men, I don't want to put you out, but I'm painting this place for Easter. So I'll have to take all our furniture outside." Having said this, the peasant and his son, a strapping lad of about 18, began to move beds, wardrobes, tables, chairs and stools out of the house. We were good sports and helped the two men. After a while we noticed that the peasant's son was no longer with us. But we thought nothing of it, because the farm was a large place and we assumed that he might have other chores to do that day besides moving furniture.

After the house had been cleared of everything that could be moved, we returned to the shed where the peasant had put us up, and went to sleep. There was nothing we could have done during the daytime; we had plans for a sorty after nightfall.

When we awoke it was early afternoon. I looked through a crack in the gate of the shed and saw a group of German soldiers moving toward the farmhouse. We took our rifles and the one machine gun we owned and prepared to leave, but then we became aware that another group of Nazis were closing in on us from the opposite direction. We were trapped. The Germans opened fire.

We did what a larger fighting force might have done; we massed into a tight bunch and then, our machine gunner in the lead, we charged into the one small gap left open by the encircling ring of Germans, and shot back. While our machine gunner kept the Germans busy, the rest of us moved toward the woods. We had made a well ordered retreat and avoided encirclement in the nick of time.

But the battle was not over yet. There was a small unit of German troops coming toward us. However, they were separated from us by a strip of open ground and they seemed in doubt as to whether they should expose themselves to our fire by leaving the shelter of the trees. Zelazny Eisenberg fired and killed one of the Germans. Caught off balance, the Germans did not react. By the time they had regrouped, we had retreated deep into the forest.

We took a count of our men, and found that we had good reason to be pleased with our day's work. None of our men had been killed or even wounded in the battle, although we had been fighting fully equipped regular German soldiers. We had heard that in similar encounters elsewhere entire partisan units had been wiped out because they did not have the capability to fight off a well-organized German attack. We had done a better job; from the moment that we resisted and opened fire, the Germans stopped being so high and mighty because, apparently, they were not anxious to fight partisans if it meant a dangerous battle.

The next day we emerged from our forest shelter and returned to Pryzcowa-Gura. We were determined to find out how the Germans had got the idea of sending a regular fighting force to this particular farmhouse. If, as we suspected, the farmer had reported us to the Germans, it was time that we taught him a lesson, for if we were to permit this incident to pass without reacting, all the other peasants would follow his example and the whole area would be spoiled for us.

As we reached the outskirts of the village we saw a boy running as if the devil were behind him. Even from a distance, he looked familiar. We grabbed him and found that our hunch had been correct. This was the peasant's son. The boy now made the mistake of his life. He started to shout that it was not he who had tipped off the Germans. His father had done that. He was not to blame for what had happened to us.

We dragged him into the woods and gave him a good beating. And then it all came out. The boy was anything but an innocent farm yokel. It had all been part of a well-thought-out plan. While the farmer kept us busy moving his furniture, his son had gone off to inform the Germans. We wanted to kill the fellow, but did not want to use our guns on him, for we knew that the sound of gunfire might attract the Germans. Unfortunately the boy began to shout at the top of his voice, and this was just as likely to bring on any Germans who might happen to be nearby. One of our men, Furman, took aim with his gun and shot him on the spot.

The Germans did hear and opened fire, but failed to hit us. We were too far away.

We were not happy about what we had done. We wanted to fight Germans, not Poles. But we had no other choice, for if we had let the boy go, he would have reported us to the Germans all over again and that might very well have been the end of us.

We buried the boy in the woods. After dark, some of our men left the woods and walked into the village, scattering notes, crudely pencilled on scraps of paper, telling the villagers why we had been forced to kill the boy.

Several days later the villagers held a memorial service for the boy in the village church. As we heard later, the sermon given by the priest on that occasion had been a most interesting one. The partisans, the priest told the assembled mourners, were not robbers but fighting men, regardless of whether they were Christians or Jews. They were human beings who wanted to live and not be caught by the Germans. Accordingly, the priest warned his congregants, if a band of partisans came to your farmstead you should give them food and shelter for the night and not tip off the Germans, at least not immediately. You could always make the report the next morning after the partisans had left. Just be sure you don't inform the Germans while the partisans are still in your house, because if you do, you will end up having trouble from both sides, from the Germans for having taken in partisans, and from other underground fighters for having reported their friends.

It seems that the villagers took the words of their priest to heart, for the next day they treated us with unusual deference and hospitality. They gave us food, clothing, and even shoes, "so you can march better," they said. However, this was not enough for some of our men. They went out on their own and, instead of asking the peasants for what they wanted, acted the part of thieves and holdup men.

One of our boys was in the habit of going out, armed with a revolver and a rifle, to hold up farmsteads in the area, demanding food, clothing and money. Luckily for him, he managed to avoid those farmsteads whose owners were in cahoots with the Germans. But even our friends did not like being held up for what they might have given us out of their own free will, and they gave us a full and angry report of his activities.

We decided that, if we wanted to be known as fighting men and not as bandits, we could not tolerate any breaches of discipline among our men. We therefore set up a court consisting of Jaeger, Sever Rubinstein and myself, to try the man. We found him guilty and told him that we would be forced to take drastic action if we ever caught him holding up farmsteads again because this would endanger the lives of all the others.

XVI

Mietek Moczar

After April, 1943, we settled down into a fairly routine existence. The Germans were far too busy now on the Russian front to deal systematically with the activities of the partisans in the hinterland. We had merged into one single unit under the command of Jaeger; I was deputy commander. But for efficiency's sake we split up into two groups to make our sorties. I led a group consisting of the former POW's from Poland while Jaeger spent most of the time with the refugees from Markuszow. But Jaeger and I were always in close touch and never far away from each other.

Franek ("Skinny") Blaichman from Kamionka proved a most helpful assistant because, unlike ourselves, he was familiar with the entire region and its inhabitants

We had "adopted" a considerable number of Jewish refugees from the ghettoes and labor camps, older men, women, and children who could not be expected to fight the Germans. These people were hiding out at various farmsteads near our base of operations. We kept in constant touch with them and for a long time supplied them with food. We told the peasants in no uncertain terms that if anything were to happen to these friends of ours, we would hold them responsible and take appropriate steps. We had made friends also with some Polish non-Jews, particularly in a hamlet called Przypisowka. Nearly every boy from that village had, at one time or other, gone out into the woods to help the partisans. These youngsters were quite a different breed from the pigheaded peasants who not only refused to help the partisans but seized every opportunity to report them to the Germans.

It was during this period that we first met Mietek Moczar, the commander of the left-wing *Armja Ludova* group of the Lublin district. When we first got the message that he was going to visit our base of operations, we assembled an audience from the surrounding villages for him to address. We felt that this move should have immense propaganda value. We told the people we invited to gather at an appointed place deep in the forest near the home of a farmer who had been friendly to us in the past. We set up an elaborate security system for the occasion to keep the Germans away. We posted guards at every entrance to the forest and spies everywhere else.

When the time came, we had a really big turnout and Moczar was duly impressed. A Communist who was to become a minister in the postwar Lublin Government, he did not behave like an anti-Semite then. But as a member of Gomulka's Government, he became responsible for the expulsion of Jews from Poland.

A tall, handsome man, Moczar was very popular with women. He turned up wearing the uniform of a Polish major. He spoke very well; his theme was that all of us, no matter what our religion, were fighting for the same cause, namely, Poland's freedom from the hated Germans, and that if only we would all work together and not squabble amongst ourselves, Hitler would go down in defeat and Poland would rise again. He told us that the Polish underground was already in communication with the government-in-exile in London where, with both British and Russian support, Polish refugee volunteers were being trained as officers and undercover agents. Moczar also informed us that we were located in an ideal spot from which to harass the Germans. Our area beyond the woods was dotted with concentration camps and also crisscrossed with highways and railroad lines. The forest in which we had our base was so dense as to be almost impenetrable to anyone who was not thoroughly familiar with the region; hence, it could hold thousands of partisans who were in the best position to harass the Germans. When it came to supplies, however, Moczar pointed out, we were definitely at a disadvantage because we were so far away from the Baltic coast. We could expect no aid from underground headquarters, and, unlike the Polish partisans, we had no homes to return to for shelter and food. Our homes had been destroyed, and, as a consequence, everything depended on whether the farmers would do for us partisans what they could; by helping the partisans, they were doing their patriotic duty for Poland.

Moczar stayed with us for a few weeks, went with us on our operations, and gave us many helpful hints. Shortly after he left, we received another visitor who happened to be one of Moczar's close friends. This man, who was known as "Bolek Alef," was a Jew who had escaped from the Warsaw Ghetto before the revolt. At that time the ghetto fighters had just managed to establish contact with the Polish underground. Bolek was their liaison man with the *Armja Ludova*. He never stayed in one place but moved from one partisan base to another. His real name was Bolchowiak, and he was short and very Jewish looking. A highly intelligent man, he had studied law before the war. At that time he was slightly older than the other partisans, perhaps in his mid-thirties, and he was instrumental in organizing the *Armja Ludova*. Today he is still alive in Poland, and active in Jewish affairs. When a delegation of Polish Jews from the United States visited Poland in 1978, he acted as a kind of liaison officer with the remnants of the Jewish community there. He has achieved very high positions within the Polish government and was for a while the Polish military attache to Washington.

Bolek warned us that our area was heavily infested with units of the right-wing *Armja Krajowa*, most of whom had little love for Jews. This, he explained, was the reason why, of late, we had begun to suffer casualties; men who went out in pairs or small groups to gather food supplies frequently failed to return. They were being picked off, Bolek said, by the "A.K."

Nevertheless, we maintained certain contacts with the "A.K." Jaeger and I often met with their leaders, educated career officers who sought recruits among the peasants. When the Polish government-in exile which had been organized in London dropped a parachutist into our area to make contact with the "A.K.," we were the first to meet him because we happened to be at the place where he landed. We found lodging for him at a farmstead and subsequently met with him again. Like Moczar and Bolek from the opposite faction, the "A.K." man gave us some good tips. However, we did not often have such encounters with the "A.K." We were wary of them because we had no way of knowing when they would turn on us.

Early in the summer of 1943 we had an unpleasant incident with the "A.K." A small group of our men, including Jaeger and myself, had gone into one of the villages for food and decided to spend the night there. Somehow, the "A.K." unit in the area got wind of our whereabouts and they opened fire on us early the next morning. We returned the fire and the shooting went on for almost half the day. I still do not understand how it was that we didn't attract the attention of the Germans. At any rate, luck was with us, and none of our men was hurt. But we wanted to find out who had put the "A.K." on our trail. We had our answer. From time to time, Poles from nearby villages would join our partisan units, going along with us for the ride. But whenever we had a run-in with the Germans, these hangers-on would take fright and vanish, because they had homes to which they could return. We, the refugees and ex-POW's, had no other choice but to hold our ground and fight. It turned out that some of these Poles were not merely cowards but also spies. The individual who had set the "A.K." on us, it was discovered, had contacts in nearly every village around us and, with the help of these contacts, informed the "A.K.," and sometimes also the Germans, of our activities.

We called on our Polish friends from the village of Przypisowka for help. They promptly came to our aid and before long we had flushed out all the troublemakers. The man who had caused our most recent trouble with the "A.K." confessed without too much prodding. We shot him right then and there, and buried him in the woods. As for the other spies, our men tracked them down to their homes, where they made short shrift of them. Some of the spies, realizing that the game was up, left their homes and made off for parts unknown.

Another time, we found that we were being followed by a group of boys on bicycles. When we stopped in our tracks and demanded to know what they were up to, they said that they had been following us because they wanted to join our unit and help fight the Germans. We did not believe them, in those days no Pole had a bicycle unless he had got it from the Germans. Therefore anyone riding a bicycle was immediately suspected of being a German spy, or at least of having contact with the Nazis. We gave the boys a proper grilling and then proceeded to beat them up. In no time at all, they broke down and told us that they had been under orders from a German task force set up expressly for spying on partisans. They said that they were not Poles but Ukrainians. This piece of information only made matters worse for them because we Jews at the time hated the Ukrainians with a fury second only to our rage at the Germans. The Ukrainians were working hand in hand with the Nazis, trying to outdo Hitler's SS when it came to torturing Jews. We were aware that, only a few kilometers away, the Ukrainians were enthusiastically helping kill Jews at the death camps of Maidanek and Sobibor.

But at the moment these young Ukrainians who had trailed us apparently had little heart for killing. They turned tail. Yet we captured them all and shot them. Zelazny Eisenberg, who was strong as an ox, picked up one of them bodily, lifted him above his head and flung him to the ground before putting a bullet through him.

XVII

Operation Markuszow

After this incident we moved to another locality, where the atmosphere was entirely different. Here, the Poles actually behaved as friends, keeping us unformed of all German movements in the neighborhood.

One night, soon after our arrival at our new base, we spent the evening at the house of a farmer. It was a pleasant interlude because the family were friendly and ready to have a good time. Suddenly the farmer rushed into the room, frightened and upset. He said he had seen a truckload of German soldiers heading toward the farm. We leaped from our benches, gathered up our weapons and took up positions at every door and window of the house. We had hardly assumed our "battle stations" when the door of the farmhouse was flung open and a German soldier shouted the farmer's name. Instantly, Franek Blaichman was upon him and shot him in the face. But the man did not die at once; he staggered out, bellowing. At the sight of his comrade, another German outside opened fire with a machine gun. Our men responded in kind from an upstairs window; the machine gun dropped from the German's grasp and clattered to the ground. Little Mikolai Berezyn darted out of the door, grabbed the machine gun, tossed it back into the house and went off in hot pursuit of the wounded German, who was still reeling about the court-yard.

Mikolai closed in on the German but the Nazi was a big fellow and the sight of little Mikolai on his back was somewhat ludicrous. Though blood was pouring down his face, the German apparently had plenty of strength left, for he lifted his arms, simply brushed Berezyn off his back as one would a bothersome insect and flung him to the ground. Luckily, Franek Levin, a cousin of Blaichman, came to Mikolai's rescue; he took aim at the German, killing him instantly. The Nazi fell across little Mikolai so that we had to drag our friend from underneath the heavy body.

We looked around for the other occupants of the German army truck. But there were no other Germans around. We teased the farmer for having panicked and warned us of a whole truckload of Germans when, in fact, the truck had contained no more than two.

Mikolai had been wounded, but it turned out to be nothing serious. After giving him first aid, we searched the area to make sure that no other Germans were about, looking for their two missing comrades. We looked for the "army truck"; it was more like a jeep than like the huge vehicle the farmer had pictured for us. We set fire to it, finishing the job by literally beating it to pieces with our rifle butts. Then we broke up camp and left for the woods near Lubartov.

Later, we learned that the second German, the one whose machine gun had been literally shot from his hand, had also been wounded. He had made his way back to the German camp but had died several hours later. The Germans raided the farmhouse and arrested the farmer despite his protests that we could not possibly have been partisan fighters.

The Germans then turned their attention to us, and put us under constant harassment. We broke up camp once again and returned to the Garbow forest, on the outskirts of Markuszow.

On our very first evening at our new base, one of our friends from Przypisowka, a Pole named Franek, came to us in great excitement. His men, he told us, had come upon a large supply of weapons which had been dropped by parachute from a Russian airplane. The find included machine guns, ammunition, hand grenades and boxes filled with special fuses and explosives.

We called in Dvoretzki, our bomb expert, who spent all that night examining the Russian weapons and planning how the explosives could be put to the best use possible. We promoted him to the newly-created rank of "bomb squad captain."

The next evening we set out for Genek Kaminsky's headquarters. We arrived at his hideout at dawn and set up camp in the woods nearby. This time Kaminsky made no move to invite us to the farmhouse where he was staying. Instead, he came to our camp for a brief talk with Jaeger, Franek Blaichman, Franek the Pole, and myself.

Genek had some important orders for us. He had received information that the Germans had been drafting all the young men of the province into a forced labor service. To this end they had compiled a register of all the young men; these records were kept at the town halls of each village. Our job was to impede the draft by destroying the registers of as many villages as possible before the Germans could put them to use. Our orders were succinct: burn down all the town halls of the province, beginning with Garbow and Markuszow.

This was no small assignment. We spent several hours with Genek, planning the operation. We told him about the Russian weapons that had been turned over to us and assured him that with sufficient forethought and preparation, we should be able to accomplish our mission. Franek Blaichman volunteered to take care of the town hall in Kamionka, his birthplace. Another one of our men, Issar, asked to be let loose in Markuszow, where he had quite a few friends. There, he said, he would have a field day roughing up any Germans or "A.K." members he might find. Genek had many important suggestions to make about timing, methods, and escape routes.

We decided that Garbow should be our first target. We sent out our spies to note the movements of the Germans in that town and to draw a layout of the town hall. Dvoretzki was busy manufacturing fire bombs with delayed-action fuses and gave us detailed instructions on how to use the weapons. Nothing was to be left to chance.

Toward evening we sent an advance party to take up hidden positions and to guard the escape routes. Directly after nightfall, others entered Garbow in groups of twos and threes. The timing was perfect. One man got into the town hall through a rear window. Once inside, he opened the back door. Two more men slipped in, closed the door again and stood guard behind it. It did not take our men long to put the bombs and fuses in position. When everything was prepared, they fired the fuses and left the building. There was no time to lose, for the fuses worked by a melting device which gave the men just about four minutes to put a safe distance between themselves and the town hall. Soon we heard the roar of an explosion, followed by the rumble of falling masonry. Looking back from the highway we could see the town hall in flames. The air was filled with the shouts of excited people and the bells of fire engines. We turned off the highway and climbed a hill from which we were able to look down on Garbow and watch the fire. We hoped that, after all our trouble, the German draft lists had indeed gone up in flames along with the town hall.

The next night it was the turn of Kamionka. We gave Franek Blaichman the pleasure of setting the bombs in the town hall there. Again, everything went according to schedule and everyone was able to make a swift getaway before the charges went off and turned the town hall into rubble.

After that, we concentrated our energies on Markuszow, which was the largest town on our list. It was also the most sensitive spot, because both the local police and the German occupation troops had their headquarters directly across the street from the town hall. Besides, except for Issar's handful of friends, most of the Poles in Markuszow belonged to the "A.K." Issar told us that one of his friends was an engineer working in the boiler room of the town hall and would be willing to let our men in through a back door at a prearranged time.

I decided that in view of the special difficulties presented by the setup in Markuszow, we would need a "dry run" to see whether we even had a chance to get near the town hall without being noticed by the police or by the Germans. I wanted to get our escape plans organized because I was convinced that we would not be able to complete this operation without a battle.

Seldom did a "dry run" go so wrong and yet have such astounding results as "Operation Markuszow." Issar began the evening by slipping into Markuszow for a secret meeting with his friends in the town's market place. Zelazny Eisenberg went with him and others. It was a market day; the market place was crowded that night, and each booth was lit by flares.

After Jaeger and I had placed our men at strategic points on the highway which we planned to use as our return route, we went on a reconnaissance tour with our newly-created "bomb squad."

When we saw for ourselves how close the German headquarters and the police station were to the town hall, we made up our minds that these were impassable barriers, not worth the risk. We therefore decided to call the whole thing off and sent one of our couriers to the market to locate Issar and Zelazny and bring them back to us.

Unfortunately, there were complications. When our courier arrived at the market place, he could not reach Issar and Zelazny because they were in the center of a free-for-all with some "A.K." men. The commotion had brought additional "A.K." men to the scene; there were wild shouts, followed by gunfire. In the confusion, Issar, Zelazny, and several of Issar's Polish friends from the town fought their way out of the square and ran for their lives, hugging the walls of the houses, and looking out for a dark alley through which they might escape.

We were still in our positions a few yards from the market place. Our courier came and informed us that we might as well give up any idea of coming to the rescue of Issar and Zelazny, because the German troops and the local police had virtually taken command of the market place.

We moved a little closer and watched the crowd. It suddenly occurred to us that with all the excitement in the market place, no one might be left inside police headquarters to watch the town hall. I grabbed Jaeger: "Never mind the dry run!" I hissed into his ear. "Let's get in and do the real job right now!" Without another word, Jaeger signaled the "bomb squad" to make for the town hall. The rest of us took our prearranged position. Within four minutes the "bomb squad" had entered the town hall with their tools, while we remained on one side of the market place, watching. What we thought had been sure failure gave every sign of ending as a smashing success, in the literal sense of the word. Franek, whom we had dispatched into the crowd, brought news that Issar and Zelazny had fought their way up an alley and that the soldiers and police were rushing to trap them.

Eventually, our "bomb squad" returned to our ranks. "Mission accomplished," Dvoretzki whispered. We now turned and moved toward the highway we had chosen as our escape route. We did not leave our posts one split-second too soon. The fuses had not been set too well, so that the bombs went off minutes earlier than had been scheduled. Zelazny was struck in the chest by a piece of flying metal as he came running out of an alley. He said he thought Issar was still somewhere in the market place. Literally lifting Zelazny off his feet, we made a dash for the alley. The crash and rumbling noise behind us made it clear that our bombs had done their work. No one even attempted to pursue us. After we had moved a safe distance from the town, I climbed a hill the better to be able to see what was going on in Markuszow. It seemed that by then all the people had left the market place and had rushed to the burning town hall. The fire brigade, probably called by the police, had arrived with plenty of noise.

Eventually Issar, accompanied by a couple of his friends, turned up. We were glad to see him alive and unhurt. One of our men who had been missing told us that he had wandered away from the market place and had stood in the crowd watching the town hall burn. We had several wounded, one killed and one automatic pistol lost.

We retreated to our forest, where we attended to our wounded. Most of those hurt were able to walk, but Zelazny, who had been hit, was in considerable pain. We assigned two of our men to take him to Drop's farm, where he stayed until he was able to move around again without difficulty. He still has bits of metal in his body, but, from what I hear about him from time to time, he is quite fit. He has been living in Israel for almost 30 years now.

XVIII

Railroad Sabotage

In the late spring of 1943, Sever Rubinstein lost his father. While his sons Sever and David, and his daughter Blimka, moved from place to place with their partisan comrades, the old man had been kept safe at the farm of our friend, the French woman who had been living in Poland so long that she never thought of herself as anything else but a loyal Pole, eager to do her bit to free the country from the loathsome Germans.

One day Sever, David and a few men from our unit went to the farm to visit the elder Rubinstein. To our dismay, we found the farm in a state of turmoil. In addition to Rubinstein, the lady of the house had given shelter to other refugees and a girl from Lublin. To the misfortune of all of us, the girl had caught typhus and had gone a little crazy from the fever. As a consequence, she had wandered off. Mindful of what she considered her responsibility for the welfare of a young girl, the French lady went out to search for her. As we heard much later, the girl must have been ever crazier than anyone of us had suspected: she had gone to the house of the district leader and given us away. She had blabbed out everything she knew: our names, and the name of the Frenchwoman. The district leader, fearful of trouble from the authorities, had gone at once to tip off the Germans.

We, of course, had no idea of what the girl had done. All we knew at the time was that she had disappeared and that her "landlady" was very much concerned about here. We stayed at the farm most of the day. Just before darkness we left. But we had not been more than half an hour's march away from the farm when one of us, turning back, drew our attention to a reddish glow in the dark sky. We immediately suspected that the glow came from the farm, and retraced our steps. We found the farm on fire. The few neighbors whom we knew stood nearby, stunned. The Germans had come, they told us, and had set fire to the farmhouse. A primitive wooden structure, the building had burned to the ground. Poor old Mr. Rubinstein and his gallant hostess had never had a chance to escape.

David and Sever were in a state of near-collapse and pleaded with us hysterically to search for their father. I had to drag the two brothers away by force, before the Germans could discover our presence.

We took David and his wife Bela and her sister Blimka to the village of Wola-Przybyskowska where friendly farmers would take care of our wounded. One of the farmers offered to give us shelter to the three distraught Rubinsteins until they recovered from the shock.

By this time we were itching to have a go at a major sabotage project, something a little more sophisticated and effective than derailing a mere freight train. Dvoretzki, our "bomb squad captain," was getting impatient. He had built himself a bunker which no one else was permitted to enter and in which he was busy night and day tinkering with the weapons and ammunition which the Russians had dropped near our base by parachute. His aim was to rig up devices for blowing up bridges and railroads. He had already constructed a land mine which, he told us, could be detonated by remote control.

"And what's the difference between your land mine and a real bomb?" I inquired.

"Simple," Dvoretzki replied. "A real bomb'll go off if you just frown at it. With my land mine you have to poke at the cord with your finger to make it explode. But I think my land mine is better."

Small wonder that nobody had any particular desire to go near Dvoretzki's bunker.

At last we were ready for the big job. Our scouts had found a good site: a place where the railway line came through a small depot and round a long bend. On either side there was a high embankment. Behind the embankment, some distance off, was the main highway. There were plenty of trees where we could post lookouts to give us the necessary signals. By this time we had concocted quite an elaborate code.

We had no way of finding out the exact schedule of the trains, but we had observed that a train came by at least once every hour. About 600 paces from the little depot at the end of the curve was a small culvert over which the train had to pass very slowly. This was to be our target spot. The time was to be early morning.

The morning was cloudy and I felt jittery. Dvoretzki had placed his land mine and run the detonation cord up the embankment. We could hear the train approaching; almost simultaneously, our scouts signaled to us that they had seen it coming around the bend. We all climbed the embankment. The train was very long and moved very, very slowly. Somewhat to our disappointment, we did not see any armored cars; it seemed to be just another freight train.

I worked my way along the top of the embankment in the direction of the little depot. I now had an excellent view of the scene. One elderly uniformed man emerged from the depot onto the narrow platform. He was followed by another man, also in a dark stationmaster's uniform. Further on, I saw a third man moving toward the signal box. As the long train came closer I saw that it included many cars covered with khaki tarpaulins beneath which we could see tell-tale outlines. The train was carrying armaments, after all. And, as if to make things easier for us, it also included two cylindrical oil tanks.

It seemed an enternity before the huge, black locomotive chugged into the depot. The driver leaned out of the cab, shouting something to the old man on the platform. The fireman waved a rag. Far in the back, at the end of the train, I was able to make out a guard car. Before that car was a low truck carrying soldiers crouched around a swivel-mounted gun. Just then Jaeger, who had joined me at my observation post, disappeared. The first trucks were passing the depot. As the locomotive moved around the bend I heard footsteps behind me. I turned and saw Jaeger, followed by a few others of his group, running in the direction of the rear of the train. Apparently they wanted to attack the truck carrying the gun and the soldiers.

Suddenly there was a great roar and a crescendo of crashing metal as the cars began to slam into each other. I could see the two uniformed men on the platform stand rooted to the ground, as the soldiers around the swivel-mounted gun fell one over the other. A weird hissing sound rent the air. Matros came running toward me. He crouched low beside me, hardly able to breathe.

"The locomotive's off the tracks," he whispered. "And the culvert, just a big hole in the ground now!" I ran with him for a closer look. Our men had left their observation posts and were racing down the embankment. The giant locomotive was lying almost on its side like a wounded monster, emitting torrents of hissing steam. Our boys had grabbed the trainmen and the fireman—both Poles—and pulled them to safety. I heard shots in the rear. There were German soldiers firing at our men, who were trading shot for shot. The two oil tanks lay directly opposite the depot. "Blow them up!" I shouted to Dvoretzki as I ran past him, along the side of the cars, for cover.

By the time I had made it half way to the forest, the shooting had stopped. One after the other, our men appeared, their machine guns in their hands. But the story was not yet over. Our lookouts were waving at us frantically, pointing to a side road that led up to the station.

"Army trucks!"

A long column of German military trucks had come to a stop on the side of the road, apparently awaiting orders from a staff car at the rear.

Dvoretzki lobbed one of his homemade hand grenades at the oil tanks, but without effect. But then came a burst of machine gun fire, and there was a deafening roar. A sheet of flame went up and a billowing column of black smoke. Another gigantic explosion followed. I was knocked flat to the ground; so were the others, nearest to me. Struggling to our feet, we raced along the railroad bed, then turned off sharply to the right and tore across the open ground. When we reached the first trees on the edge of the forest, we flung ourselves to the ground, utterly spent.

From this safe vantage point we were able to see the first German army trucks pulling up at the depot. Soldiers were jumping from the trucks and speeding toward the wreckage. None of them seemed inclined to look for the saboteurs. Perhaps it did not occur to them that we might still be around. I saw a couple of officers climb the embankment and looking through binoculars toward the northern side of the road ahead. Probably they had seen the tracks made by Andreiev and Jusiek on my instructions. They never looked our way.

We now backed out and, breaking up into several smaller groups, we made off according to plan, dispersing widely.

We had done a good day's job; one whole German armaments train wrecked, a culvert blown up, and two oil tanks set afire. The two men we had rescued from the locomotive begged us to let them go. "We're only engine men," they said over and over again, in Polish. "We don't know what was on the train. We don't know anything. There's nothing we could tell you." But Franek from Przypisowka paid no attention and shot them. We gave the same treatment to the German soldiers from the truck with the swivel gun; they pleaded for mercy but we made short order of them and then took their uniforms. We were badly in need of German uniforms for our future operations.

We were rather pleased with ourselves; we had never imagined that we would be able to do so well. But we had no time to stop and congratulate ourselves. We knew that before long the Germans would be on the lookout for us and we would have to get away quickly if we did not want to be caught. We kept on the move all that day and throughout the night that followed. By the next morning, we were close to exhaustion. I proposed that my own small group should look for a farmstead and stop there for a rest. Before long, we saw a likely place. We knocked at the door and were invited in at once.

Inside we settled down to an impromptu party as we usually did after a successful operation. We always carried in our baggage a supply of sausage and vodka, obtained as gifts, or loot, from affluent farmers, in which we indulged only when we had cause for celebration. Some of our men had a real passion for vodka, but we all knew that we could not afford the luxury of getting drunk. It was too risky to take chances on falling asleep and having the Germans take us by surprise.

100

XIX

Hanka of the Warsaw Ghetto

While we were passing round the vodka and feeling in a rare convivial mood, we became aware that we were not the only guests on the farm. Five others, four men and a girl, had entered the room quietly and were standing around watching us. I passed the bottle to the girl, who seemed to be in a state of complete exhaustion though she still managed to look attractive. "Thanks," she said, in a strained and husky voice, and handed the drink around to her companions. Our hospitable farmer made the introductions. The girl was called Hanka; one of the men was named Halpern, and the other three were brothers by the name of Rock. They were all Jews from Warsaw, who had escaped from a deportation train bound for Treblinka.

After these newcomers had been slightly revived by some food and drink, the girl and I went outside and sat down on the banks of a brook that ran near the farmhouse. There she brooded quietly for a long time, gazing moodily into the surface of the water, her hands busily playing with the ears of one of the farmer's dogs. Slowly and, it seemed to me, with excruciating effort, she began her story and that of the four others who had found shelter at the farm together with her.

101

By the latter part of February, 1943, Hanka told me, everyone in the Warsaw Ghetto had sensed that some terrible change was about to take place. By early April, 1943, it had become obvious that the Germans were going to liquidate the ghetto, either by starving all the Jews to death or else by persuading them to leave the crowded ghetto for "work farms" in the surrounding countryside. Many of its 200,000 Jews had fallen into the Nazi trap and agreed voluntarily to move to the "work farms," but before long reports had filtered back into the ghetto that the volunteers had all been taken directly to the death camps. From that time on, Jews had stopped "volunteering" for service on "work farms" outside the ghetto. Thereupon the Germans had changed their tactics. Every day, they arbitrarily ordered Jews to report to the *Umschlagplatz* or assembly point where trucks would be waiting to take them to places of work beyond the ghetto walls. Many of the men and women assigned to these "outside work details" were never heard from again.

About a year before, Hanka continued, inmates of the Warsaw Ghetto had banded together to form a "Jewish Fighting Organization." The commander of the organization was a young man in his early twenties, Mordecai Anilewicz. A member of a Zionist youth movement before the war, Anilewicz had continued his Zionist organizational work even inside the Warsaw Ghetto. In addition, he had made frequent trips outside the ghetto, at the risk of his life, to establish contact with surviving Jews in other Polish cities. In January, 1943, he had led his men in several brief skirmishes with the Germans, and during the weeks that had followed, he had organized those Jews still in the ghetto for the final battle. On April 19, 1943, the ghetto was invaded by regular German armed forces, who brought up tanks and heavy artillery to shell and bomb the ghetto into submission. Within hours, the ghetto was ablaze. Women, children, the elderly and others unable to join the active fighting hid out in basements or improvised shelters. Those who crept out of their shelters in an attempt to escape from the ghetto were immediately caught by the Germans or Ukrainians who had joined the German troops in the all-out attack on the Jews. In either case, the unfortunates were gunned down on the spot. The scenes in the ghetto defied description. Young people, including rabbinical students, who had never even touched, much less used, a rifle before, fought the Germans from the burning rooftops with guns smuggled in from friendly Polish underground bases and with crude, homemade Molotov cocktails. Anilewicz commanded his men directly from fighting positions and from his headquarters at Mila 18. When the Germans finally surrounded that building, Anilewicz flung himself from the roof to his death rather than surrender.

The Germans made a house-by-house search of every building that had not been burned or shelled into rubble. In one of these buildings they had come upon Hanka, Halpern and the three Rock brothers. The five had been trying with primitive tools to force open a trap door through which to escape. When the Germans burst into the house, Hanka and her friends managed to hide their tools inside their shirts but they were unable to elude capture. The soldiers seized them, dragged them out of the building and flung them onto waiting trucks. They were driven at once to the railroad station where a long train of box cars packed with other Jews from the ghetto had been lined up. They were thrust into one of the box cars and the door was rolled shut behind them. Moments later, the train pulled out of the Warsaw station. Someone near Hanka whispered that the train was headed for Treblinka. The mere mention of the death camp was enough to make Hanka and her four friends mute with sheer terror.

The human beings crammed into the box cars received neither food nor water. Daylight came in only through narrow cracks between the wooden slats of the box car. There were no seats, no heat, and no toilet facilities. By evening, it was bitter cold, and the air was foul with the stench of urine and excrement. As the long slow journey progressed, panic broke out. People began to scream hysterically; many fainted and some died of heart failure.

Luckily for Hanka, Halpern and themselves, the three Rock brothers did not succumb to hysteria. They worked their way to the door of the box car and, with the small tools they had saved from the Germans, began to cut and saw away at the heavy bolt that sealed the car, and at the wood around the bolt. All night long they worked, taking turns at a task which seemed hopeless. At long last, miraculously, it seemed, they got the door sufficiently open to pass one arm through. After several more hours of work, they succeeded in loosening one of the cables that had been tied around the bolt. The cold night wind outside numbed their hands as they labored, but finally they had cut away enough of the rope and wood to open the door of the box car to about twelve inches.

The train was traveling alongside a river at top speed. The three brothers, along with Halpern and Hanka, squatted close to the door hoping that, sooner or later, the train would slow down so that they might be able to jump off with some chance of survival. They knew that if they waited too long, they would not be able to escape; if they passed through a station, the open door with its ropes hanging loose would soon be noted and reported. Hanka stared out at the river which reflected the night sky. Presently she saw the lights of a bridge straight ahead. The others, too, noticed. As it approached the bridge, the train slowed down. Hanka and her friends knew that the bridge would be heavily guarded but they felt that this might be their last chance to escape before daybreak. Without hesitation Hanka pushed herself through the opening in the door and jumped from the car. She hit the ground and rolled over and over. The four men followed her. Luckily, except for some bruises, none of them was hurt. They kept moving until they reached a wooded area where they felt safe from capture. For several days they moved southward and eventually came upon a farmstead. The woman at the farm gave them warm jackets and some food but her husband, the farmer, would not permit the fugitives to stay at his house. He did not want the Germans to catch him giving shelter to people like that, he told his wife.

The five moved on and came to another farm where they were accorded the same welcome. Some food, yes. But shelter, no. Finally, one of the farmers had brought them to the place where we partisans were staying. "That farmer has guts," he had declared admiringly. "He takes in your kind. We're not that brave. You might as well try him." And so they had.

That was how I met Hanka. She told me outright that she intended to join the partisans together with her male companions, and that she did not see the fact that she was a girl as any kind of obstacle.

I told Hanka that our group would move on that night and that she was hardly in a condition to go with us. "Why not stay here for a while and get your strength back?" I suggested. "These farmers are decent people, so you should be safe here. Your four friends can come along with me. We won't move too far away, so that you can follow along later.''

"I'm in no worse state than they are!" she said sharply. "Even if I am a girl. I tell you, I can also fight; I'm able to handle a rifle and am as good a shot as any man. And I'm willing to work, to get at those beasts!'' Her eyes flashed. "I didn't come here to be pampered or treated like a lady!" she declared emphatically, and there was nothing I could say that would stop her from following us. Reluctantly, I gave in. There simply was no time to argue, since we had to get as far away as possible from the site of the train we had sabotaged.

That night we left the farm and made a long night's forced march. Hanka loped along beside me like some jungle animal, completely fearless, and I could not help admiring her high spirits. She was little more than a skeleton but even so I could tell that she was a beautiful woman. Her eyes were very dark and deep. Finally we stopped at another farmstead, at a sufficient distance from the site of our "operation," where we were able to relax for a few days.

It was in the seclusion of the forest, during this short respite, that Hanka and I became close, and our relationship continued, punctuated by constant partings and reunions, until the end of the war. Despite her very high-spirited and assertive manner, Hanka was a very warm and passionate woman. Although she was far from docile she listened to me when I advised her for the second time to stay behind with her friends for the time being. "You won't think I'm saying this *now* because you're 'only a girl,' '' I reproached her. "It's just for that reason that I'd like to have you with me. But it's *you* I'm concerned about. You'll never be able to keep this up." I told her firmly. "You have to eat, rest, and put some flesh on those bones before you can travel with me. I'd like to see you fill out a little! Don't worry! Do you think I'll forget to send for you? But first you have to get back into shape. In your condition, you would hinder us more than you could possibly be of help.''

This final argument seemed to convince Hanka at long last, and she and her four friends agreed to remain on the farm.

XX

Vagaries of Our Work

Our group continued moving further and further away from the scene of the train wreck. According to reports we received from Lublin, the train incident had infuriated and alarmed the Germans because they had not considered that part of the country "dangerous" before. Now they launched a concerted clean-up operation to rid the forests of "bandits," as they called the partisan fighters.

To add to our troubles, we were hit just then by a series of misfortunes for which we could blame neither the Germans nor hostile Poles. Issar, one of our best fighters, lost his life in a stupid accident. One of our men had wrested a Russian pistol from one of the A.K. men. None of us had ever seen such a gun before and everyone wanted to see it. One of our men, standing guard in front of the farmhouse where we had set up temporary headquarters, wanted to examine the gun at closer range. He picked it up without knowing that it had just been loaded. Before anyone could warn him, the gun went off. The bullet passed through the man's palm and then hit Issar, who was standing nearby. Issar was killed instantly.

Several weeks later Furman was wounded in a freak accident. One of our men who was cleaning weapons dropped a loaded pistol; it went off and the bullet hit Furman in the stomach. Perhaps, with prompt medical attention, he might have survived, but doctors were a scarce commodity in partisan units. Furman lived only a few days after the accident. We buried him in the marshes.

We had in our unit a young man who happened to be a cousin of Franek Blaichman. Somehow, this young man had got hold of a bicycle from one of the farm boys in the area, and took to riding around on it. As I have already said earlier, bicycles were not often seen about those regions during that period. It was unusual for a Pole to have a bicycle unless he had obtained one from the Germans, mostly for the purpose of carrying on espionage activities for the hated Nazis. And so it happened that one of our men, seeing Blaichman's cousin from a distance riding on a bicycle, mistook him for a Nazi spy and opened fire. Luckily, the man's aim was not accurate, and Franek Levin was only wounded in the arm. We took the poor fellow to the house of our friend, Drop, which by this time had become something of an emergency hospital and convalescent home for our wounded. The wound was very serious, and Franek Levin never regained the full use of his arm.

From that time on, we instituted a set of very strict rules to prevent future accidents involving the careless use of weapons. First, I gave orders that all guns should be kept loaded at all times so that it should never occur to anyone to handle a gun with anything but the utmost care and respect. Furthermore, I instructed my men never to allow their weapons out of their sight. They were to wear their weapons on their persons at all times except when they slept, and even then, they had to keep them close by. The cleaning and inspection of weapons was turned into an orderly, disciplined operation. All the cleaning was to be done by the entire group together, at a set time, the first thing in the morning, according to a stringent routine, with each man turning over his weapon to someone else for inspection. I hoped that, given such stringent regulations for the care of weapons, accidents of the kind that had taken the lives of Issar and Furman would never happen again. Of course I must add that, throughout the gun-cleaning procedure, several lookouts would stand on guard with their own guns, and one machine gun would be kept at the ready, so that our men would not be overtaken and wiped out by German raiders while they were busy cleaning their guns.

Shortly after this stroke of ill luck, we received word that Mietek Moczar, head of the Lublin district of the *Armja Ludova,* was ready to pay us another visit. We were advised to stay in one place for a few days so that Mietek should have no trouble finding us. During this "stationary" period, Hanka, Halpern, and the Rock brothers caught up with us. They insisted that they were now in fine shape and ready to take part in our operations. I asked Jaeger what I should do about the four new recruits. Jaeger was all for our keeping them with us. Accordingly, I told Hanka and her friends that they had been accepted into our unit. Hanka was the first girl to enter the all-male unit, though later other women joined her. The division of labor, however, was still into the conventional man-and-woman roles. The girls still did the cooking and the housekeeping chores.

We had become quite proficient at living in the woods, though we had had to learn it the hard way. We had learned to find our way at night by the stars, whenever the sky was clear enough for us to see them. We were able to tell the North Star from the Great Bear. I remember being lost one night with some other men. I wondered which direction was east, and which west. One of the men in our group was a huge Russian, who had joined us after escaping from a German POW camp. He went up to a large tree, put his strong arm around its trunk and seemed to caress it lovingly. I found his behavior a little strange until he extended his arm in one direction and declared emphatically, "This is east!" It seemed like witchcraft until he explained that when the trees were wet, the daytime sun, shining from the south, dried only one side of the trunk. Accordingly, if one's palms were sensitive enough to moisture, a few gentle pats of the trunk could establish quite clearly which side was north and which south. Once you knew that, you were also able to tell which way was west, and which east.

We would keep all our food in one big sack which we would take turns carrying. No one liked this chore because such a sack could be a real impediment if one suddenly had to run from an approaching German patrol. Andreiev, the enterprising young man

Relaxing after a skirmish.

who had traced the inhuman shrieks of our first night in the forest to the wind sighing through the bough of a tree, particularly detested being left to carry our food sack. Whenever his turn came to tote the sack, he would think up a thousand excuses to weasel out of the job. This calls to mind an incident which had its humorous side but which I took very seriously at the time it happened.

We had spent a day at a farmhouse where we had been given a good welcome and where there were some good-looking girls. All that day, Andreiev had avoided carrying the sack, insisting that the others were foisting the job on him when, in fact, his turn had not yet come.

That night we had a good time with plenty of drinks. An ex POW who was not bad-looking was devoting his complete attention to one of the farm girls. Suddenly a courier brought me a report that a German patrol was on the move and coming in our direction. However, the Germans were still a long way off, and I decided that we were safe for the moment because the Germans did not, as a rule, patrol the forests during the night. But I passed word to all our men to be prepared for a very early start the next morning. The farmer's wife had gathered food for us and before long our sack was repacked and ready at the door of the farmhouse.

Just before daybreak we assembled in the courtyard and said good-by to our hosts, the men only, because the women had not cared to come out in the dark. I looked around for the sack with our food. The sight of the sack reminded me of our comrades arguments the day before. Where, by the way, was Andreiev? He was not out in the courtyard with the rest of our men. Where could he be? He knew that we had to move off. There was no time to lose, for once it was day, the Germans would begin their pursuit. Furious, I rushed back into the farmhouse and charged up the steps. Still no sign of Andreiev. Then I heard low voices. The sound came from the kitchen annex. I flung open the door and there, on a bed in a corner, I saw him, with a girl all but wrapped around him.

"Hey you!" I roared. "What are you doing here? I mean, why aren't you up yet? We've left already." I realized that what I had said did not make much sense. Confused, and embarrassed at the poor girl's shrieks, I turned tail and fled down the steps.

In the hall below, I met the farmer's wife. After a few quick words with her, I rejoined our men in the courtyard. There, much to my surprise, was our Andreiev. He must have dressed with lightning speed to have got there before I did. I gave him a proper lecture in front of the others for endangering the lives of all of us by not obeying orders.

Then I shouted to the men, "Let's go!" and led them out of the courtyard.

After we had marched for some time I heard muffled guffaws behind me. I turned to see what was so funny. What I saw was our Andreiev, dejected, with our food sack on his back. Thus laden, he was trudging along, his head bowed in penance beneath the weight of his burden. In the midst of all our troubles, I could not help laughing.

But although Andreiev's liking for girls had its comical side, it was unfortunately to prove his downfall, for it was after such an

110

expedition to meet some village maiden for a rendezvous that our comrade disappeared. We found Andreiev's body thrown out on one of the village streets, and that was the end of our high-spirited comrade.

XXI

Winter 1943-44

The rest of the spring of 1943, and the summer that followed, passed rather uneventfully. The Germans were increasingly engaged with the Russians on the eastern front, so that they seemed to have little time or heart left to deal with the partisans behind the front lines.

The winter of 1943-44, like the preceding winter, was bitter cold, and we were snowbound for weeks on end. Many of the operations which we had planned could not be carried out. But early in January, 1944, Mietek Moczar, accompanied by a group of *Armja Ludova* men, reappeared and gave us new orders. We were to move out of the area where we had spent most of the preceding year, to cross the River Wieprz and then to make for the Parczew woods. While the rest of us began preparations for the move, Mietek borrowed some of our men for a special mission: to teach a lesson to a gang of Ukrainian and Lithuanian collaborators who were ambushing partisans in the village of Jamne. The men picked for the mission included Sever Rubinstein, Franek Blaichman and Bolek Alef, the Warsaw Ghetto fighter. I did not go with them myself, but they gave me a full report when they returned. There had been a full-scale battle, in which many of the Germans and their collaborators were killed. None of our own men had been

Moczar and a small group of partisans preparing for action in the Parczew woods. Seated in the second cart is Samuel Gruber.

hurt. Bolek Alef was furious with Mietek because one machine gun had been lost in the fighting, and Mietek had placed the blame on Bolek, calling him "negligent." Bolek resented Mietek's attitude and said he wanted nothing more to do with him.

In February, 1944, we started moving toward the River Wierpz. We split up into two groups once again, the one under the command of Jaeger and the other led by me. Jaeger was sent out to locate two Russians who had been parachuted into the area from a Russian plane. These Russians had radio equipment with them and were in constant touch with Moscow. Unfortunately Jaeger had no chance to accomplish his mission. He ran afoul of a German patrol and was killed. It was a great loss not only for our unit but also for me, personally. I had come to respect Jaeger as an able leader and a brave fighter, and missed him greatly. Sever Rubinstein was hit in both legs. He was taken to Wola-Przybyslowska, where he stayed with his sister Blimka. Somehow, the two managed to elude capture. We met again in Lublin after the liberation.

Luckily, the first encounter with the Germans resulted only in

113

these two casualties. But we were not yet rid of the Germans. When the group, now under my command, stopped near the River Wieprz, we found ourselves surrounded by Germans who had emerged behind us and from the backs of the houses close by. The Germans were cutting off our retreat; our situation seemed hopeless. We made a leap for the river banks. The banks were several feet high; we used them as a shelter from behind which we returned the enemy fire, holding the Germans at a distance. The banks of the river ran along open ground. A little further upstream, there were a few low wooden piers. Our men on the right wing, edging along in that direction, came upon a small rowboat. While others kept up a covering fire, these men grabbed hold of the boat and pushed it upstream, unnoticed by the enemy because of the river banks. At a spot better shielded from view, they climbed into the boat. Vladek Laks, a cousin of Issar's, a short, blond fellow from Markuszow, took the oars and rowed back and forth three or four times, until all of us had been ferried safely to the opposite eastern bank, right under the noses of the Germans. It was an extraordinary performance, especially in view of the fact that all this took place in broad daylight. We had with us on this expedition some Poles from the *Armja Ludova,* most of them from the town of Przybybowska, whom Mietek had sent to us. One of them was wounded in the fighting on the other side of the river, and he later died. He was our only casualty.

At the same time Mietek sent us word about a new mission. A group of Polish officers had "come down from heaven" not far from us. Translated into more down-to-earth language, this meant that troops from a Polish army-in-exile, organized in the Russian-occupied sector of Poland, had been dropped by parachute from Russian planes near us, well behind the German lines. These men had with them an ample supply of weapons, including machine guns, but they had landed on the "wrong" side of the Wieprz and had been pinned down by the Germans. They would not be able to hold out indefinitely. Our orders now were to re-cross the river to the west bank, find them and get them across quickly to our own side.

In the mist before dawn we readied the rowboat in which we had made our original crossing and moved it upstream. I do not remember the names of all the men who went on this mission with me, but I recall that the group included Zelazny Eisenberg and Stefan Finkel. We took with us a long rope which we hurriedly put up as a primitive pontoon. This is how all the men from Russia managed to cross the river. The only casualty among them was the commanding officer, a man named Janowski, who was seriously wounded and had to be carried across on Zelazny's shoulders.

Janowski was properly impressed with our feat. He assured me that he would send a report of our herosim to Moscow and that all of us would be decorated. It turned out that Janowski was Jewish. After the war, he became the publisher of the most important newspaper in Communist Poland.

That night we moved to a village where we stopped to make a roll call. But we knew that we would not be able to spend the night in the village; together with our new comrades-in-arms from Russia, we were too large a body to be overlooked by the Germans. To remain in one spot for more than two hours at the most would give the Germans time to send reinforcements, against which we would not be able to hold out.

We marched all that night. Suddenly we were stopped by a man in a Polish officer's uniform who seemed to have been waiting for us behind the trees. He told us that his name was Kolka, that he was Mietek's right-hand man, and that he would take charge of us. He was familiar with the area, he said, and would guide us to a place where we might set up camp without fear of being attacked by the Germans, at least for the time being. Unfortunately, as far as we were concerned, Kolka started out on the wrong foot. He kept addressing us not as "men," but as "Jews." All the time it was, "Come here, Jews!" "Go there, Jews!" "Stop, Jews!" and "Forward, Jews!"

Finally I got tired of Kolka's behavior and said to him, What's all this business about 'Jews, here' and 'Jews, there'? What kind of a Polish officer are you, anyway? We may be Jews, but we're partisans of the *Armja Ludova,* just like you. So kindly stop calling us 'Jews.' If you can't call us 'men,' then don't call us anything. But stop the 'Jews' business, if you want to stay out of trouble!"

All the time I was talking to him, Kolka had been sitting on his horse and had not bothered to get down. He had not so much as blinked an eye, just sat tall in the saddle and said not a word.

I grabbed him, dragged him from his horse and set him on his feet, facing me eyeball to eyeball. I told him that if he knew what was good for him, he would henceforth mind his manners. We were not in the habit of laying our hands even on those contemptible individuals, Jew or Gentile, whom we discovered to be collaborating with the Polish Fascists or with the Germans, but if he, Kolka, would not behave himself and treat all our men with the proper respect, we would give him a beating he would long remember.

Kolka got the message, and from that time on he was as good as gold. He took care not to insult us again and we even became friends after a manner. But I never lost sight of the truth: Kolka was a dyed-in-the-wool anti-Semite and could not be trusted with the welfare of Jewish partisans. Unfortunately there was no way of ridding ourselves of him, because he reported directly to Mietek Moczar.

Kolka was killed in the 1960's when he was shot down in a plane flying over North Vietnam.

XXII
Harassing The Germans

One morning in the late winter we arrived at a village near the town of Ostrov, not far from Lubartow. There we came upon a whole army of partisans, Poles and Russian ex-POW's, who acted as if they were the rulers of the land. They had horses and even army trucks, and they moved about freely. They hardly ever suffered casualties. The Poles in this area were different from those I had encountered in the past. Actually, they were not pure Poles but Byelorussians; they were bitter enemies of the Germans and eager to help all partisans, regardless of whether these happened to be Gentiles or Jews. They gave us food and found us lodging for the night for many weeks, without ever asking us for anything in return.

Several days later we met a group of Jewish partisans under the command of Yechiel Greenspan, known as Chil for short, about whom I had heard many great stories. He was an energetic, plain-spoken man who showed no deficit in common sense. He was a splendid comrade-in-arms with a great zest for life, good high spirits, and a healthy appetite for what are known as the "good things of life." Joseph Rolnick, a young man in his twenties, and Chil were the only ones in this group to have served in the Polish army before the war. Like me, Chil had held the rank of corporal.

Chil Greenspan and his most active partisans.

Nobody else in his group had experienced any military training before they entered the ranks of the partisans. The group was made up of Jews from neighboring villages, along with Jews who had jumped from trains bound for the death camps or who had escaped from the camps themselves. Chil was extremely popular with all of them. Like some gallant hero of a ballad he freely roamed the woods and did not hide in bunkers. Far from hindering him as an interloper and a Jew, the local populations lent him their assistance so that, unlike my men, Chil's group was well-equipped with horses and with weapons supplied by the peasants.

Chil led us around the area so that we might become familiar with the terrain. The Parczew woods were much older and thicker than those to which we had been accustomed west of the River Wieprz. Deep inside the thickest part of the forest there was a clearing where more than a hundred Jews, women, children, and old people, were gathered in one great camp, fed and protected by Chil's partisan unit.

Before long, our men began to grumble about the unfairness of their lot. The other partisan units in this area had horses, carts and army trucks, they pointed out, while we were forced to carry out all our missions on foot. Some of our men volunteered to go back to our former bases west of Wieprz, raid some of the more affluent farmers and take the horses. But I was very much against the idea, because I felt they would be risking their lives for no good reason. Still, a large group of our men disregarded my advice and went out to look for horses. They took some fine saddled horses from one rich landowner and set out to rejoin us. But on the banks of the River Wieprz they had a rough encounter with the Germans who had lain in wait for them there. The exchange of fire went on for hours and many of our men were killed, including Vladek Laks, who had ferried us across the river, and Vladek's best friend, Ettinger, who had come from a well-known religious family in Markuszow. Vladek had a brother who survived the war and is now living in Israel.

The partisans were now regrouping and forming larger units around Lubartov and Ostrow, under Mietek Moczar's command. Mietek's inner circle included a number of Jewish men who had been well known in Poland's literary and artistic world before the war. Chil and I, though in command of different detachments, were beginning to work together very well. He knew every corner of the terrain, and I made it my business to let him teach me as much as possible. I felt that you might as well know the geography of the terrain in which you would have to do the fighting.

The first joint project on which Chil's unit and mine collaborated was the wrecking of a railroad bridge on the line that linked Chelm, Lublin and Warsaw. The line ran from Lublin across the River Wieprz, due east to Chelm, from there to the River Bug, east to Kovel and the battlefront. The bridge we chose crossed the River Wieprz; the main highway was about five kilometers to the north. While we busied ourselves with "preparing" the bridge, one group was dispatched to a vantage point from where they could watch the highway for German military convoys.

We arranged matters so that we would get to the bridge and plant our mines just before a train was due to pass. In this way we planned to kill two birds with one stone, as it were. Dvoretzki, our "bomb squad captain," placed the mines, this time not homemade explosives but sophisticated land mines which had been parachuted to us from a Russian plane along with other weapons. We were now much better equipped for our work; we had even acquired some horses from nearby farms.

119

Having completed "preparing"the bridge, Dvoretzki, the others and I remounted our horses and proceeded to a point on the highway some distance ahead. Then we turned off into the woods and stopped briefly to study our map. At that moment we heard a roar and the shattering noise of metal crashing against metal. We had hit our target. Later we learned that the train had run right over the mine and plunged into the river in a flaming mass, along with a sizable complement of German soldiers who had been on their way to the battle front. The mission was a big success; the Germans put their losses in the hundreds.

The next task at hand was to make the main highway unsafe for German military traffic. Night had fallen and I could scarcely see in front of me. I had been riding on a white horse at the head of my party; after a while, however, I had become tired of riding, gave my horse to another man, and began to walk in the direction of the underbrush at the edge of the woods where I hoped to get a good view of the main highway.

I stood beneath a solitary tree, looking to my left where I could see the distant main highway run from west to east. Suddenly I became aware of a large, dark square mass just ahead of me. It was a truck standing still and silent. The others dropped flat to the ground and I found myself so close to the truck that I could not even move. And then I saw something else: a German soldier aiming his gun almost straight at me. It flashed across my mind that in the darkness he had not noticed me but had caught a glimpse of my white horse which was perhaps about fifteen paces back of me among the trees. If I made one false move, the German would see me and shoot. The other men lay on the ground unmoving.

I had been carrying my rifle not in my hands but over my shoulder. The problem now was how to move it into aiming position without the German noticing that there was anything moving in front of him. I lowered the gun to my side, inch by inch, and gradually tilted it forward in my right arm without moving my left side. The slightest additional movement would only have increased the chance that the German would see me and put an end to my labors. At last, stopping gently, I got the rifle into position in my hand and prepared to fire from the hip by moving my other hand across almost at the speed of light until I could hold the gun in my left hand and slide my right hand back to the trigger. All this took only seconds, but it seemed like hours and though the night was cold I could feel the sweat run down my face.

But once I had the gun in shooting position I decided that I was now in control of the situation.

"Put down your gun, soldier," I whispered to the German in his own language, "You are surrounded!"

The expression on the man's face was downright comical. He looked up into the trees, then slowly turned his head this way and that, and at last slowly lowered his rifle.

"What are you doing in this place at this late hour?" I asked him. He told me that his truck had broken down.

"Are you alone?" I demanded.

No, he replied, there were four others. Two of them had gone to the nearby village for help. Another two were asleep in the cab of the truck. At my signal, my men , rifles cocked, rose from the ground and moved toward the truck. They opened the door of the cab, and presently there emerged two huge Germans, their eyes wide with amazement to find themselves looking down so many rifle barrels. One of them wore the black uniform of the SS; the other, the green uniform of the Waffen-SS, which was part of the regular German army.

The truck was loaded with radio equipment and sophisticated weapons, including a new kind of ten-shot machine gun I had never seen before. The soldier in the SS uniform explained that he had taken it from the battle front. We pulled our three prisoners back into the woods and I sent a party of our men to the village to find the other two. We pushed the truck up a narrow lane in the woods where it could not be seen from the main highway.

We worked half the night stowing away the weapons from the truck and then taking the truck apart, piece by piece. All the time we kept a sharp lookout for the two other Germans who had supposedly gone off to the village, but out men returned from their search empty-handed. We never did find out what had happened to these two Nazis.

We turned our attention to the three Germans we already had in hand and gave them a thorough interrogation. They seemed tired and depressed. One of them told us that the battle lines were very close by, and that the German armies had been suffering one defeat after another on the eastern front. In all likelihood the Germans would move an entire army corps into our area to fight off a Russian drive on Warsaw. Our prisoners were thoroughly disillusioned with the war and with their military leaders. The General Staff, one of them said, had let them down. The man in the Waffen-SS uniform agreed but put much of the blame on the Nazi High Command which he said had been interfering with the generals' business. Our third prisoner asserted that the fault lay with the Nazi bigwigs in the immediage entourage of the Fuehrer. "The generals lose only battles," he spat out bitterly, "but we ordinary soldiers lose our lives." All three, however, agreed that Germany's precarious military position was not really Hitler's fault. The trouble lay in the fact that the unfortunate Fuehrer had surrounded himself with the wrong men.

I recalled a scene that had taken place about two years before: a visit of SS chief Heinrich Himmler to our camp at Lipova 7. We had been locked into our barracks for the occasion but through the windows we were able to catch a glimpse of the man, surrounded by a mob of Nazi big shots. He looked such an ordinary, mean little creature, I wondered how men like him could possibly run a big country like Germany. But soon after he had gone, new anti-Jewish measures were announced, and promptly executed, in Lublin. So these leaders must have had followers, after all. Was I really to believe that the robots who had followed Himmler and his henchmen so blindly had now changed their minds and were beginning to blame the Nazi generals for Germany's troubles?

We searched our prisoners, and stripped them of their documents, maps and other military equipment. Then we took them back with us to Chil and his men. We did not know what we should do with them. And so we dragged them with us from village to village, trying to have them put up at the same farmhouses where we ourselves took shelter for the night. But none of the farmers wanted to take in Germans. They were convinced that the German army would be searching the area for our captives and that if these men were to be found at any of the farmhouses in the area, all the farms would be laid to waste and the farmers massacred.

We wandered about for a week with our German prisoners in tow. There was no way of communicating with Mietek Moczar to ask his advice, because we had learned that the German army was scouring the woods all around us for partisans. But we could not drag the three Germans about with us forever. Finally, Chil and I sat down to decide what should be done about them. We came to the obvious conclusion that we had got all the information we could from them and that their presence in our unit posed a threat to our lives since their friends would certainly be looking for them. We therefore agreed that they would have to be disposed of as quickly and as quietly as possible. The Germans had never hesitated to shoot their Jewish captives; why, then, we reasoned, should we have any compunctions about giving the same treatment to our German prisoners? When we informed them of their fate, the three German soldiers lost their composure; they burst into tears and begged for mercy, promising to do whatever we wanted, even to fight on our side. But their act did not help them. We shot all three and buried them in the woods.

XXIII

Working the Highways

Several days later we were finally able to make contact with Mietek Moczar and eventually to reach his headquarters. There, we found a new man, a Jew in uniform who, we were told, had been parachuted into our area from a Russian plane. Born in Lvov, he had been a career army officer even before the war. His real name was Skutnitzky, but he had adopted the surname Zemsta, because he had had no particular desire to be known as a Jew.

When we told Moczar and his advisors about our German captives, the initial reaction we got was cold fury. Why, Moczar shouted, did we decide the Germans' fate on our own without consulting him? We should have brought them to him for questioning no matter what the risk. He accused us of having carelessly disposed of three valuable sources of first-hand information on what was transpiring at the battle front. But after we had explained to him that there had been no way for us to get in touch with him, and that we were sure we had obtained all the information our captives had in their heads, Moczar relented and even complimented us on the fine job we had done wrecking the truck.

We continued "working" the highways, going out in groups of twenty men to harass German trucks and military cars bound for the front. Our guide in this operation was a man named Korn, who was born in Parczew and was supposedly familiar with the terrain. Unfortunately it turned out that he did not always know where he was going; accordingly, Yurik Cholomski, who had been in Chil's group together with his father and brother, took over the job. Both Korn and Cholomski survived the war and are now living in the United States.

The "highway jobs" entailed considerable risk because the Germans had observation outposts from which they kept the highways under close surveillance. Nevertheless, our very first day was successful. We hid behind trees, and when the first German army truck appeared, we darted out from our hiding places and surrounded the vehicle. The first man to reach the truck was Lonka Feferkorn, a member of Chil's group. He, too, was from Parczew.

The crew of the truck turned out to be Poles, not Germans, but the truck was filled with cases of whiskey, cigarettes and other goodies intended for the German soldiers on the battle front. We forced the truck off the highway, but since the side roads which led to our base, an abandoned house in the village of Kodeniec, were not negotiable by truck, we had to use a horse-drawn cart to transport our captives and our loot to the place we wanted them. The transfer of the goods from the truck to our primitive cart took quite a while. Suddenly, a Polish fellow who looked about 18 materialized out of nowhere and offered to help us. We took him up on the offer and started to talk with him while we worked. The Pole began to ask us some questions of his own, which sounded suspicious. We therefore took him back with us to Kodeniec and had him subjected to our own brand of interrogation. In the end, he broke down and admitted that he had been working for the Germans. He had been ordered to trail us and to report to German headquarters whatever he might be able to learn about our present activities and about our plans for future operations. He told us the names of a number of Polish peasants who, he said, had also been spying for the Germans. We immediately sent out a group to round up the peasants. It took us days to question them all, but we found that our young Pole had told us the truth; these peasants had been maintaining steady contact with the Germans and had given them information about partisan operations in the area. We let most of the peasants off with a good beating and a warning of worse to come if we ever caught them working for the Germans again. But our young helper was less fortunate; we felt he knew much too much. We therefore convened a court-martial and sentenced him to be shot. We buried his body behind the house that served as temporary base for our unit. It was a horrible thing to do. As Franek and I walked away from the fresh grave, I remarked to him, "To think that when I first took to the woods, a farmer once gave me a chicken and asked me to kill it and I couldn't bring myself to do it. And here I've killed a man!"

"Well, you were in no danger from the chicken..." Franek ventured.

"I know, I know," I interrupted him, "But it makes me sick."

XXIV

From Partisans to Soldiers

In April, 1944, Russian planes were over our area again, dropping about 70 uniformed Polish officers from the Russian occupation zone, with plenty of weapons and ammunition. A large number of these men were Jewish, but only two of them made a point of identifying themselves to us as fellow Jews. One of these two eventually fell in love with a pretty girl from Holland who had joined our unit after escaping from the death camp of Sobibor. The parachutist was almost constantly at her side. Unfortunately, her sufferings at the concentration camp had left her weak and ill. Eventually, she could no longer walk. We therefore had to leave her behind with some other comrades when we moved on. We later learned that she was caught by the Germans and killed.

Shortly after the arrival of the parachutists from Russia, one of our men, Lova, went out with a small group to find some food in a neighboring village. The peasants whom they approached turned out to be members of the *Armja Krajova*. The other men managed to beat a hasty retreat, but Lova was beaten so severely that he collapsed on the highway in a pool of his own blood. He lay there until some friendly peasants came upon him, recognized him, and brought him to our base. His condition was so poor that we did not see how he could possible survive without medical care. Then,

127

Hanka, the girl from the Warsaw Ghetto, offered to stay with him and guard him until he was better. So we said goodbye to each other, knowing that it was our duty to offer our services where they could be put to best use, and that we had to sacrifice our private feelings to the cause for which we were working. Mingled with the intense attraction I felt for Hanka there now was respect for the decision she had made. So when the rest of us moved on, she stayed with Lova in the woods. I caught a last glimpse of her standing alone, her slender body leaning slightly against the door of their shack, waving to us with a peasant-woman's shawl she used to tie back her hair. I really did not expect to see either of them again, but somehow both nurse and patient survived. After the liberation, we found them where we had left them, both of them in very bad shape. We moved them to Lublin where they were given medical treatment and eventually recovered. Somehow, after the war, Hanka's and my paths diverged. Like me, she remained in Lublin for some time, and had a top job as a secretary in the city hall. But it was not the same between us as it had been as partisans in the forests. Our interests differed and we could not fit each other into our new life-styles. Hanka is living today in Tel Aviv. She married a cameraman who worked in Israeli Television. She has a daughter, and is now an exclusive dress-designer in Tel Aviv.

All through the year 1943 the Ostrow area had been a hotbed of partisan activity. With the help of the officers who had been parachuted from Russia, the Polish partisans had set up a true military base, well-stocked with Russian weapons. However, the Poles and Russians did not merge into one unit but retained their separate identities. Accordingly, Bolek Alef, Chil and I decided that the Jewish partisans in our area should cease operating as small bands dispersed among the non-Jewish groups and organize into an all-Jewish unit. We Jews wanted to demonstrate that we, too, constituted a national entity, with particularly good cause to desire the downfall of our common enemy. Chil was appointed commander, I was deputy commander, and Franek Blaichman and Dvoretzki (the bomb expert) were platoon commanders. We would continue to report all our activities to Mietek Moczar at his headquarters but, except for special missions which Moczar might assign to us, we were to plan our own operations, no longer as bands of partisans but as well-drilled, well-armed soldiers.

Whole family units like the Rubinsteins who had managed to escape together from the ghettoes or from the death trains and had joined the partisans liked to fight alongside one another. Among the followers of Chil, for instance, there was the Pomeranc family, consisting of two brothers and one sister, Jurek, Pacan, and Cesja, who were fond of talking about a brother Jac, an active partisan on the left bank of the Bug River. Pacan, our youngest partisan, was about 12. My first sight of him was when he pranced proudly into camp on a huge black horse. He looked very pleased with the dashing figure he was making but, unfortunately, as his mount careered around, it caught its hoof on a bump in the ground, tripped, and threw its young rider. Not only was Pacan down, but he was just picking himself up in great mortification when the horse swung round and administered a resounding whack on his head with its hoof. I carried the unconscious boy to the nearest farm and hung over him until I was relieved to see the eyelashes flicker. The fall from the horse was a real blow to his pride, but otherwise, he was not hurt. Another family, also connected with the Pomerances and fighting in Chil's troop were the Cholomskis, consisting of an aunt, Chancia, a father, Abraham, and a son, Yurek, who made constant reference to Yurek's brother, Mordecai, who was fighting with Jack Pomeranc on the other side of the Bug.

The most active members of Chil's group were Dudkin, Rolnick, Lonka, Politruk, Adam Winder, David Friedman, the Abarbanel brothers, and several others. Now, for the first time, we accepted girls as something more than a necessary evil in partisan ranks. Hanka was no longer an exception. Each smaller unit in our company had a girl or two who helped in the cooking and the other housekeeping chores at our base. Some, though not all, of the girls even had guns. Roska and Dora had weapons of their own and knew how to use them. Roska is now living in America; her husband is Yurek Cholomski, who acted as our guide in our "highway operation." Dora eventually became Chil's sister-in-law; married to Chil's brother, she is now living in Brazil.

At long last, the top echelons of the Polish underground movement were beginning to take us seriously. We were not only receiving parachutists and sophisticated weapons from the Russian zone east of the River Bug, but were entrusted with important missions

129

A group of partisans posing for a rare picture. Back row, center, is Dora.

that were part of a grand design of resistance and sabotage operations planned by Polish exiles behind the Russian lines. Sometimes we received visits from leaders of the Polish left-wing underground movement who were based in the Russian zone. Among these prominent visitors were a number of men who were to occupy key positions in postwar Poland, including Osovka Morawsky, who was to become Prime Minister in the Polish government set up by the Russians in Lublin. At the end of one such visit, Zemsta Skutnitzky, the career officer, informed us that Osobka Morawsky and two of his colleagues, Hanniman and Spychalski, had to proceed at once on a secret mission to Moscow and that a Russian plane was waiting for them at a secret landing site on the Russian side of the River Bug. Zemsta asked me to assign to our visitors a hand-picked group of fighters who could escort them across the river with dispatch so that they would not run afoul of the Germans on the way and the plane would be able to take off with them aboard before the Germans could get wind of their presence.

130

My choice fell on Franek Blaichman, Zelazny Eisenberg, Vladek, Morel and several others whose names I no longer remember. The party started out on schedule, but when they arrived on the western bank of the Bug, the border between the German and Russian occupation zones, they encountered German soldiers and armed Hungarians who were fighting alongside the Nazis. Luckily, our men proved their fighting prowess; they successfully fended off the enemy. Our charges were unhurt and arrived safely on the other side of the river. They reached the plane without delay and took off for Moscow. On their way back into the German zone, our men again successfully eluded the Germans and, though some of them had been wounded, they all made it back under their own power. No one had been killed.

In April, 1944, we were able to save two Jews from execution, not by the Germans or collaborators, but by trigger-happy Polish partisans. It had been reported to us that a Polish partisan unit had captured a married couple who had been spying for the Germans. We hurried to the scene and got there just as the two "suspects" were about to be led to execution. When I got a closer look at the man, I recognized him at once. He was Jusiek Cynowiec, one of the Jewish prisoners of war from the Polish army who had been with me at Lipova 7. I also recognized the woman; she was his wife. Jusiek was wearing a Polish army jacket. The Polish partisans told me that they had found him and his wife hidden at a farmhouse near Ostrow and that both had been found guilty of pro-German espionage. I asked the Poles to hold everything until after I had talked to Mietek Moczar. I rushed off to Moczar and, with some heat, told him that these two could not possibly be German spies. When he finally satisfied himself that Jusiek and his wife were personally known to me as victims of Fascism, he gave orders for their release. The Cynowieczes then joined our unit and remained with us until the end of the war. They eventually settled in Haifa, where Jusiek became an officer in the Israeli army.

In our movements through the woods during the latter part of 1943 and the early months of 1944, we encountered increasing numbers of fellow Jews who had escaped from nearby death camps. They had come from many countries, Germany, France, Belgium, Holland, and Russia. Some of them could speak neither

Polish nor Yiddish but only German. Others spoke neither German nor Yiddish but only French or Dutch. Among the escapees of Dutch origin was the attractive girl who stole the heart of one of our Polish officers. She, a young man named Vladek, and Atleta (not identical with Vladek Laks, one of the "old-timers" in our unit) had escaped from Sobibor, where some 250,000 Jews eventually were to lose their lives. She told us the story of the inmates' revolt that had taken place at this death camp on October 14, 1943. The uprising had been part planned, part spontaneous. The cobbler's and tailor's shops of the camp which, of course, operated with forced inmate labor, happened to be next door to each other. It was arranged to have the two highest SS officers in the camp visit the shops at the same time. The camp commandant was in the tailor's shop trying on a jacket that was being made for him, while his deputy was at the cobbler's getting some boots repaired. Inmates armed with axes burst into both shops at the same time and split the skulls of the two distinguished "patrons."

The sudden death of the two top Nazi officers threw the entire camp into confusion. The inmates literally went berserk. About 150 Jews, Poles, Russians and Dutchmen, rallied behind a fellow inmate, Saszka Pierczerski, and led an organized revolt. A mass escape began. But before long the Germans recovered from the initial shock and gave chase with machine guns. Many of the inmates were killed, but a considerable number were able to hide out in the woods.

One day, Vladek, one of the survivors of Sobibor, sat talking with one of the young men, a non-Jew, in the Polish unit. Both were holding their rifles. The conversation turned to the possibility that the Germans might overrun our partisan base and that, if we were not killed, we would probably all be taken to one of the death camps. Vladek said that rather than go through such an experience again he would pull the trigger and shoot himself with his rifle.

"I'd just put the muzzle under my chin, like so, and press the trigger with my foot," he declared, and as if to emphasize his words, he thumped the ground with the butt of his rifle. There was a loud report; the rifle jumped with the recoil and the bullet struck the young Pole beside Vladek, killing him instantly.

Naturally, we had to go through the formalities of investigating the incident. Of course, Vladek was cleared, but from that time on we Jews sensed that, though they never said as much, the Poles looked upon us with mistrust.

Later, we received into our unit refugees from the death camp of Treblinka. Most of the Treblinka survivors were too sick or too badly hurt to help us in our operations. We therefore set up a camp for them in the woods near Ochorze where they would have a chance to recuperate, and we took it upon ourselves to guard them against German raids and to supply them with the food they needed. For some reason the camp became known by the name of Tabor.

There had been an inmate uprising in Treblinka also, and on a much larger scale than at Sobibor. The inmates, many of them survivors of the Warsaw Ghetto, seized the camp arsenal and used the explosives to blow up the gas chambers. The camp was turned into a battleground. Many hundreds of Jews were killed, but an impressive number escaped from the camp and made for the woods nearby.

By that time we had a regular courier system through which we were kept informed of developments throughout German-held Poland and were able to pass on the news. In this manner we learned that anti-Nazi revolts were taking place not only in the death camps but also in Cracow, Czestochowa and Bialystok. These uprisings were brutally quelled but not before much damage had been done to the enemy and hundreds of Jews had managed to flee to the countryside and go into hiding.

Early in 1944, we had to cope with unrest in our own ranks. Chil had been getting reports from friendly peasants in the area that young boys from Camp Tabor were roaming the countryside, foraging for food. Since it was generally known that we partisans had assumed the care of the concentration camp survivors, the peasants felt that we owed them compensation for whatever was taken by these lads. Chil felt uncomfortable, because many of youngsters involved hailed from his own home town near Parczew. He therefore kept his distance and asked me to go to Camp Tabor and give them a proper talking to.

I took a few of my close comrades with me for moral support. Conditions in the camp were beyond belief. The men were going about half naked. The crude shelters that had been set up for them offered little protection from rain. The people slept on straw

133

pallets without any blankets. Food was cooked over campfires. I called all the refugees together and spoke to them. As I looked at the men, women and children before me, I noticed one woman who looked exactly like my mother. She was not my mother, of course, but the resemblance was so striking that I was unable to tear my eyes away from her as I spoke.

I launched into a lecture. I told my listeners that the tide of battle was beginning to turn and that the Russians would soon drive the hated enemy out of Poland. But it was our task to help hasten the end of Nazi domination, and the success of our fight against the Germans depended in great measure upon them, the concentration camp survivors in Tabor. Whether or not we partisans would be able to carry on effectively depended on our ability to retain the good will of those peasants who were not at present collaborating with the Germans. These peasants, I explained, were plain, decent people who had frequently helped us out with food and other supplies. But if we, or the Tabor refugees, would begin to raid and loot the farmsteads, this would antagonize the peasants. Therefore, the raids and forays which the young people from the Tabor camp had perpetrated could not be permitted to continue. If we were to lose the good will of these Poles, our usefulness as partisan fighters in the area would be at an end. We were therefore going to rely heavily on the older men and women at Tabor to restrain their young people so that we would be able to keep the friendly peasants on our side.

As I spoke, I kept staring at the woman who looked so much like my mother. My memories of my parents and my old home town almost overpowered me, so that I had difficulty completing my speech. But this was not the time to surrender to emotion. I dismissed my audience, except for the young people, mostly teenagers, whom I now began to lecture in earnest. I reprimanded them for having brought the wrath of the local peasants upon us by their inexcusable conduct, and I warned them impressively that in the future anyone caught poaching would be severly punished, perhaps even shot, as an example to the others.

The youngsters stood before me in silence, looking very solemn. I turned away and, followed by my comrades, went back to the partisan base.

XXV

Poles and Russians

In May, 1944, we received word to expect a visit from Rola Zimirski, commander-in-chief of the left-wing *Armja Ludowa.* Our instructions were to inform not only our own men but also the Polish peasants in the vicinity and arrange a gathering at which Zimirski might speak. Zimirski, a non-Jew, had been a career officer in the Polish army before the war. Now, he was in command of the left-wing underground movement, but he was definitely not a Communist. He was also known to sympathize with Jews and their problems.

We went all out to give Zimirski a royal welcome. Our unit even issued a bulletin in honor of his visit. It was only a handbill, crudely lettered in pencil, but I would like to think that its contents made up for its primitive appearance. I was the editor and contributed an article about the place of women in the partisan movement. I criticized those units which still refused to take in girls. Girls, I pointed out, had the same rights as men and had proven to be useful members in many partisan groups. My article was much discussed and earned me the approval of the girls in our unit.

Zimirski was greeted by a large crowd. Peasants from Ostrow and the entire Parczew area had gathered in a clearing in the woods to hear him. They were impressed that the commander-in-

135

chief of an entire movement, left-wing or right-wing made little difference to these simple souls, should have expressed the desire to meet with them. They got their money's worth. Zimirski had arrived well prepared, even bringing a photographer to take pictures of the scene, and he gave the audience a rousing oration. Suddenly we heard a drone overhead. It was a lone German plane, flying rather low. But apparently the pilot of the plane did not think there was anything unusual going on, for he continued on his flight and nothing untoward followed.

Zimirski was interested in every phase of our activities, but particularly in our Jewish unit. He shook hands with everyone, including the girls. He asked many questions: Where had we come from? How did we divide our duties? Did we have any news of our families? And finally he called over his photographer and posed for pictures, quite a few with Chil and myself.

The next day he issued an order promoting Chil, Franek Blaichman, Dvoretzki and me to the rank of lieutenant in the *Armja Ludowa*. A number of other men from our Jewish unit were given non-commissioned officer's rank in Zimirski's army.

Zimirski called a conference of officers from the Polish and Jewish partisan units. He told us that the area was no longer safe for us. The Russians were very close; if we stayed, we would soon be caught between the advancing Russians and the retreating Germans, and we all would probably be wiped out. Our orders, therefore, were that we should return to the region from which we had started out originally, the Vistula river area, just west of Lublin. This meant passing through familiar terrain in the direction of the Garbow woods.

The Polish partisans accepted these order with equanimity, but we Jews were very much disturbed, because we knew from past experience that the Poles living in the Vistula river region hated the Jewish people. Chil and I met briefly with our own people. The consensus of opinion was that we Jews should not go along with Zimirski's instructions, but stay right where we were. Quite aside from all the other considerations, there was Camp Tabor to think about. It would be impossible to subject these concentration camp survivors to the long trek west, and we could not very well leave them behind. The forest was large and in some places almost impenetrable; surely, there would be places where we would be able

136

to hide out without fear of being caught in a battle between the armies of Russia and Germany.

We went to Zimirski and told him our opinion. We also spoke with Mozar and Zemsta. We argued that the Jewish unit could perform a valuable service to the other partisan unit by staying behind as a rear guard after the others had moved westward. Zimirski and Zemsta finally accepted our proposal, but insisted that at least a small contingent of our men, who knew the terrain, accompany the Polish unit on its way west. Among those who went west were Franek Blaichman, Mikolai Berezin, Yurek Cholomski, and two girls, Hanka and Roska. Zimirski left, too, for an unknown destination. About 100 of us, under the command of Chil and myself, remained behind in the woods near Parczew.

Several days after Zimirski's departure, we received a message by courier from the rival underground movement, the right-wing *Armja Krajowa,* that they were taking over the entire region. They

Chil Greenspan and Samuel Gruber (1944).

requested our unit to merge with them and take our orders from them, or else face annihilation as a band of outlaws. Knowing the "A.K." and its attitude toward Jews, we naturally refused to join them. However, our rejection of the "A.K." ultimatum meant that we now had no other choice but to leave the area where we had fully intended to stay until the end of the war.

Some time before, we had heard that a unit of Russian parachute troops was operating in another sector of the Parczew woods, under the command of a general named Boronowsky. Later, we learned that Boronowsky was not a native Russian but a Hungarian Jew. But we did not know this at first. Before moving our entire unit, or what was left of it, we decided that Chil and I should go to the Russians ourselves and make personal contact with Boronowsky. We made the journey on horseback, taking with us a young survivor of Warsaw Ghetto named Rubinstein (no relation to Sever). This Rubinstein, a short fellow, was left-wing oriented; that is why we used him as the "political officer" of our unit in our dealings with the Russians. Traveling on the highway, we experienced the unpleasant surprise of being machine-gunned from a low-flying German aircraft. We leaped from our horses and ran back into the woods for cover. After the plane had left, we emerged from hiding. It took us some time to find our horses, but we did find them eventually, no worse for the scare, and continued our journey to General Boronowsky's base.

We found that the Russian base was quite large and well-organized. After passing various challenges we were taken to Boronowsky, a short, fat man. He had with him a bird that looked like a parrot and a woman whom he introduced to us as his wife. He received us very kindly, even offering us caviar which he explained he had brought with him from Russia. He told us that he and his men had been parachuted into the area by Russian planes to work behind enemy lines, and he now invited our entire unit to join his company. After a while we left him and returned to our own base to bring Boronowsky's message to our men. Our unit made the journey to Boronowsky's base in regular army style. Well-armed with rifles and machine guns, and marching in perfect order, we impressed the Russian general as seasoned soldiers.

Boronowsky gave us a short welcoming speech. One of his first instructions was that our men should be "integrated" with the soldiers in his own unit. He did not want us to continue as a separate "Jewish" entity, because this was contrary to his ideology. Russians, Poles and Jews, he explained, should work together for the cause that united us all. Besides, he argued that by thus becoming part of a Russian company, we would escape the threat of attack from the anti-Semitic "A.K.", which by then was roaming the woods at will and was constantly on the lookout for Jewish partisans.

Boronowsky seemed genuinely concerned for our welfare. In addition, he apparently trusted us more than he did his own comrades in arms. Only a few days after we had joined his company, he sent for Chil and me and informed us that he needed our help in a confidential mission. He had in his possession some vital, top-secret documents, which had to be sent back to Moscow. The couriers chosen to carry the documents would have to cross the River Bug to the Russian side, where a Soviet aircraft would be waiting to fly them to the Russian capital. In Boronowsky's view, we Jews were more trustworthy than his own men; he therefore wanted us to assign two men from our former unit to take the role of couriers. The choice fell on Chil and our "political officer" Rubinstein. They were accompanied across the river by an escort of 20 Russians and one Pole, who would know the places where the river was sufficiently shallow to be crossed on foot.

Boronowsky ran his company with an iron fist. He frequently punished insubordination by executing the offender, and did the shooting himself. Several days after Chil and Rubinstein had left, he received special orders from Moscow to organize a new unit of the *Armja Ludowa,* which, of course, had to be composed entirely of Poles. The recruits included peasants from neighboring villages, and, of course, ourselves. I was made temporary commander of the "A.L." unit, which eventually grew to 100 men, and was stationed at Wola Vereszcynka, a village consisting mostly of large farms.

A few weeks after our arrival at the village, the Germans attacked. It was the first time we found ourselves in full-scale battle with a unit of the regular German army. As the Germans advanced upon us we kept up a steady barrage of gunfire but retreated into the forest. We then worked our way around and emerged from the woods at a point some distance away, retreating again as soon as the Germans noticed our presence. Before long, the Germans brought aircraft into the battle, whether it was to bring in additional soldiers or whether it was only to take away the wounded, we were not sure. One of our men happened to have with him a Russian anti-tank gun; he opened fire and scored a direct hit, for we saw the plane go down some distance away. This new weapon had been the source of contention, because it was so heavy and was therefore a nuisance when quick movement was the order of the day. But during this battle with the Germans the Russian gun more than proved its worth to us because its range was much greater than that of ordinary machine guns.

The Germans now attacked with artillery fire. I was behind a tree with a very thick trunk. Before the tree was a small puddle. A shell came whistling in my direction, but it dropped into the puddle and never exploded. This was fortunate, for otherwise I would not be alive today.

The fighting continued throughout the day, until nightfall, when it became so dark that nobody could see anything. At that point, to our great joy, the Germans simply pulled out and left us to our own devices.

During the battle, our unit had split up. One group, with Boronowsky in the lead, had gone off into the woods. Now we wanted to rejoin him and the others, but we had no idea where to find them. After some hours of marching through the night, we decided to head for the village of Kodeniec, where we had once set up a base and where partisan groups were likely to make contact with one another. Much to our astonishment, we came upon our friend Chil. What was he doing in Kodeniec? He was, after all, supposed to be on his way to Moscow with the top-secret papers entrusted to him by Boronovsky. But Chil had never made it. He told us the whole sad story.

While we were fending off the Germans at Wola Vereszcynka, Chil, accompanied by our "political officer" Rubinstein and an escort of 20 Russians and one Polish guide, had been scheduled to cross over to the Russian banks of the River Bug where Chil and Rubinstein were to board the waiting Soviet plane. Their march to the river had been uneventful. After nightfall, the Polish guide led them to a shallow point where they were to cross the Bug. The Pole was the first to step into the water. Rubinstein followed but the next moment began to scream in sheer terror, for a towering wave swept both him and the Pole off their feet. The Pole had vanished. Rubinstein attempted to swim but was unable to hold himself above water. His shouts for help on seeing the Pole drown had brought the Germans to the scene; a German border patrol had been stationed in a bunker nearby. Suddenly there was gunfire from every direction. Chil himself reached the river bank just in time to see Rubinstein go under. The Germans kept on shooting, and Chil and his men had no other choice but to make a fast retreat. So they had returned to Boronowsky, who, Chil told me, was not far from Kodeniec, and reported to him that he and Rubinstein had been unable to carry out their mission, and that Rubinstein was no more. Luckily, the most important papers destined for Moscow had been on Chil's person so that most of the documents had been saved.

Chil informed me that the situation on the German-Soviet battlefront had become chaotic, that the woods were now full of German soldiers and that we were in fact surrounded. We finally got hold of Boronowsky, who instructed us to lie low in the woods and plan no further operations until the battlefront had stabilized. Meanwhile, the Polish A.L. group had formed a new separate command under Kolka, the officer who had so infuriated us by addressing the Jewish partisans as "Jews" rather than as comrades. Kolka had sent a message to Boronowsky, asking that our group be separated from Boronowsky's Russian unit and return to his, Kolka's, command. Boronowsky was more than ready to let us go, for he had just received orders direct from Moscow, that he was not to keep any Poles, Jewish or otherwise, under his command. His was to remain an all-Russian army unit. And so we parted company with Boronowsky.

The small detachment of Jewish partisans from Chil's group that had made its way westward together with the Polish and Russian partisans had also been engaged in a direct confrontation with the Germans.

It seems that the party under the command of Zemsta and Mietek Moczar, accompanied by a large force of Russian ex-POW's, had crossed the River Wieprz and proceeded to the village of Dombrova, to clean out a nest of "collaborators." There, they had run into a detachment of Germans. Heavy fighting ensued and they had been able to beat off the Nazis. But by the time they got to the town of Romblov, the found that the Germans had followed them there, tipped off, apparently, by Polish farmers in the Dombrova area. Romblov was situated on open ground, and the partisans were exposed to German bullets, first from the air and then from tanks and light artillery. The partisans were required to take on the German army, with the German air force in full command of the skies. Our men were armed with Russian equipment, and even had some anti-tank weapons, but it was obvious that, despite the heavy casualties on both sides, the Germans were slowly closing in on the partisans. The planes succeeded in hitting the horses and wagons carrying our supplies and in killing our people. The fighting lasted all day, escalating into one of the major combats in which the partisans engaged regular troops. Among the wounded on our side was Mikolai Berezyn; he was shot in the face and bears the scars to this day. That night he was carried away by his comrades under heavy fire, together with the other casualties. After the war, he settled in Israel.

Captain Zemsta.

When it grew dark, the partisan leadership decided that, to avoid heavier casualties, they should not make a direct bid to escape through the enemy cordon that surrounded them, but that they should divide into small groups and each try to make a breakthrough. Moczar and Bokel Alef, the Warsaw Ghetto fighter, went separate ways and got through to the Janowski woods, but Zemsta, who headed a group of partisans, was not so lucky. They had set out to rejoin the group led by Chil and myself, which had remained behind the Parczew area. Zemsta's unit in fact managed to get out of Romblov and, a few hours later, came to a farmhouse, where they settled down for the night. Unfortunately they woke up the next morning to find the whole place surrounded by Germans. Zemsta was shaving when he heard the rumble of approaching tanks and the rat-tat-tat of machine-gun fire. Yurik Cholomski and Roska, who were also there at the time, saw Zemsta walk out into a direct hit, a shell bursting right in front of him, killing him instantly. That Yurik, Jusiek, Roska, and a few others succeeded in escaping at all was nothing short of miraculous. They managed to get back to Chil and me, told us of the losses we had suffered and described the heroic fight put up by the unit.

XXVI

Liberation

With Kolka now in command of a separate all-Polish A.L. unit, A.L. headquarters sent a colonel to take charge of our detachment. The new commander started giving orders at once. On the very first day he commanded all our Jewish girls to move to the woods of Ochorze, stay there for the duration of the war, and not travel about with the men. Chil and I did not like this and had a word with the colonel. (To this day I am sure that he was Jewish but did not want it to be known.) We explained to him that our girls really had no place to go and that some of them had proven to be able fighters; they had rifles of their own and had been using them to good advantage. We did not want these young girls to be pushed around, and we told this to the colonel in no uncertain terms. In the end the colonel gave in and rescinded the order. So the girls remained with us.

Whatever the colonel's shortcomings, laxity in discipline was not one of them. He had two Russian soldiers executed without courtmartial for raping a woman from a nearby village. The woman—she looked about 70 years old—had come to the colonel the morning after the incident and identified the two Russians who she said had attacked her during the night. After a brief questioning of the culprits, the colonel asked for volunteers to act as an execution squad. When no one volunteered, and the colonel was about to make his own selection, a good-looking man stepped forward. He was wearing an old, Waffen-SS uniform and had a machine gun in his hand. "I'll be glad to do the job," he said. This was Janek, a Czech who had deserted from the German army earlier that spring of 1944. Armed with his machine gun and accompanied by his girl friend, he had come straight to partisan headquarters and announced that he was through with the Germans and now wanted to join in the fight against the Hitlerites. Our usual procedure in such cases was to shoot the man because we had learned by sad experience not to trust so-called "deserters" from the Nazi armies. But Janek was a Czech, not a German, and we therefore decided to take a chance on him.

We were in luck; he turned out to be so reliable, and we had used him for a number of jobs that had to be settled with dispatch. Anyway, he now offered his services as executioner, and was quickly accepted by our colonel. The colonel called out all the soldiers to the execution site to witness the proceedings. The old lady, too, was invited; she got quite upset and cried bitterly because it had never occurred to her that the colonel was serious about having these two young men shot. The two Russians cried, too, and begged for mercy, but the colonel's only answer was to give Janek the go-sign. And that was the end of the two Russians.

Meanwhile, the battlefront was moving closer and closer to us. The Russians were advancing with lightning speed and the Germans were in full flight. We were warned that the Germans would concentrate their energies on combing the woods for partisan units to clear the path for the retreating German forces. The first limitation of these maneuvers was the frequent appearance of German aircraft flying low over the trees, obviously in search of partisans below. We were kept moving from one place to another, playing hide-and-seek with what remained of Hitler's *Wehrmacht* on the Eastern front.

We now turned our attention once again to "railroad jobs"; trains were constantly on the move near us, rushing new German troops to the battle line. One day a small group of our men, including Janek in his old Waffen-SS Uniform, placed land mines at strategic spots on the railroad tracks not far from our base, then hid behind some trees to wait for results. Dvoretzki, our "bomb expert," had joined us for the occasion; the land mines we used were his creations and he was in a state of ecstasy about them.

Everything went according to plan. It was a train packed with German troops. As usual, the locomotive fairly leaped from the tracks, and as the cars crashed into each other we saw men thrown clear out of the cars, most of which had been open trucks. Some of the cars merely turned over and the soldiers were tipped out like so many heads of cattle. Many of them still had their weapons and started shooting aimlessly. They could not aim at any target, because we kept well out of their sight, except for Janek. That fearless Czech in his SS uniform mingled with his former comrades-in-arms, his machine gun blazing away left and right. The Germans could not understand what was happening to them; that one of their own SS men should be shooting at them was something they could not grasp, and before they could begin to understand, Janek had helped quite a few of them die for their Fuehrer and Fatherland. He seemed to enjoy himself hugely, for when he finally returned to our base, he was laughing his head off. After the war, his girl friend, the one who had accompanied him to our camp, denounced him for having killed Jews before joining us. He was tried by a Polish court, and served a term in prison.

After this incident, the Germans came in great numbers to the Parczew woods and occupied every farmhouse round about. We had to hide out in the woods for days on end and could not even go out to look for drinking water or for food, which was running low.

One town the German troops occupied was Ostrow, which at one time had been a partisan base. Shortly before, we had sent Dvoretzki and some of the Jewish contingent to infiltrate among the Germans and to prevent their taking over, but without success. We had done this by order of a new commander sent from the headquarters. The colonel who had been such a fanatic on the subject of discipline had been relieved of his post and replaced by an officer named Grigori Korczynski. Korczynski was a fine soldier, but we had heard stories about him that we did not like. Although he had fought on the Communist side in the Spanish Civil War, the story now went that wherever Korczynski came, there the Germans came also. What was certain was that the man had no love for Jews. In the 1960's he was publicly brought to trial by the Polish

Government for the murder of the forty Jews who had made the first bid for freedom from the barracks at Lipova Street No. 7.

When Dvoretzki and his group got to Ostrow, they ran straight into German tanks and artillery. They didn't have a chance and made a strategic retreat. Meanwhile, all the peasants from the surrounding villages came to us and asked angrily why Jews had been sent out to fight against the Germans. They did not like the idea of our turning their area into a battlefield, for they were convinced that, after the fighting, the Germans would burn down every last farmhouse. Korczynski replied he had sent the Jews because he considered them good fighters and also because he trusted them. But our impression was different; he had sent us to do the dirty work in order to incite the peasants, who would then blame the Jews for having provoked the Germans into burning down the farmsteads of decent, law-abiding Poles.

After some days of hiding out in the woods with our food supplies dwindling fast, we decided that things could not go on that way and we would have to spring the German trap. We contacted Korczynski and he agreed to hold a meeting with Chil and myself the next day so that we might draw up plans for a break-out. But when Chil and I turned up at the appointed place the next day, we found that Korczynski had cleared out for parts unknown.

With Korczynski gone, it was up to Chil and me to plan our getaway. This was serious business. Our chances for getting out from the German encirclement were as good as nil, but we were convinced that something would have to be done, or else we would either slowly starve to death or be crushed by the Germans in the end. We decided to try a special formation, something like a flight of birds in echelon, about seven men to each echelon, and break cover in that way. However, this attempt ended in failure because the moment our vanguard came within sight of the German lines, the Germans opened fire, forcing us to dart back. I ordered a fast retreat to the left, and well back into the woods before the Germans would have a chance to shoot into the woods with their light artillery. We got away just in time. We reached a far point in the woods and then stopped, having been told by our scouts that this area was still clear of Germans.

But all this was just a temporary solution. We had to break the German ring because we had no more food left and had been reduced to drinking water from puddles. We decided that it must now be every man for himself. After dark, each man was to try to crawl through the enemy line alone. In this way, at least, some of us would succeed in getting out.

At a given signal, the first men left. We lay low beneath the trees, waiting to see what would happen, as, one by one, our "advance guard" crept out of the woods into the open terrain. We held our breaths, expecting a burst of German fire at any moment. Seconds dragged by like hours. But nothing happened. One by one, our other men moved forward, wriggling out into the darkness, then vanishing. When I myself had started on my way, the sky seemed to clear a little, enough for me to see that the man directly in front of me suddenly rose from the ground and loped forward at a good speed. Before I had a chance to wonder about the man's sanity, another man had come up on one side and hissed to me:

"You can stand up. There's no one around. The Germans have gone." I suspected a trap, and so we continued crawling on our bellies for a while. But then we, too, ran forward. There was no gunfire; indeed, there was not a sound. I could see that our men were now standing up straight at the edge of the trees ahead. The Germans had really gone. It seemed like a miracle. I sent several men out along the edge of the forest to see where the Germans might have gone so fast. After all, large forces had been there only a few hours before. They returned to report that there was no sign of the Germans. Apparently the battle front had come so close that the Germans had been ordered to leave us alone and concentrate on the Russians.

We marched to the nearest village and got some food and milk, bread, eggs and cheese. Since we had been on a near-starvation diet for quite some time I saw to it that the men did not eat too quickly or too much. I knew that too much food after a fast could cause serious illness, even death.

That evening we went to Kodeniec, our old hunting ground, and stayed there for a brief rest. Presently, we noted that all the peasants in the village seemed to be on the move, driving their cattle and horses before them into the woods. We stopped one of the peasants and asked him what in God's name they all were doing. The peasant explained that they wanted to hide their animals from

148

the Germans, who were out in great numbers collecting all the cattle they could find.

The peasant was right. The Germans were roaming the area, no longer as a well-disciplined army but more like unorganized, marauding robber bands.

In order to avoid running afoul of the Germans, we found ourselves being driven east, toward the unit under the command of Boronowsky. We knew that the woods were no longer safe for us, the German infantry was hiding out there in small pockets and if they caught us now, there would be no retreat. We decided to abandon our horses and to camp out in the open corn fields during the daytime, leaving us free to retreat in any direction if the need arose.

This was to be one of the greatest days of our lives — July 21, 1944. The corn in the field was full grown but not yet ripe for harvest. We were lying flat in the middle of the field watching German troops searching the edge of the woods to our left from where we had come. Their backs to us, they were moving alongside the trees, going in and out. I was afraid that the Germans might find the horses we had abandoned, and track us down after all, but I quieted my apprehensions with the thought that the horses had probably wandered off deeper into the woods where there were ample patches of good grass for them to eat.

We spent the entire night of July 20 in that cornfield. It was a night we would never forget. Whenever we meet today, be it in a hotel in the mountains, at a convention in New York, or at a reunion in Israel, the talk inevitably turns to that summer night in 1944. It was a night of torrential rain, such as none of us could remember ever having experienced before. The rain had begun in the afternoon and continued throughout the night, and we could not leave the field to take shelter beneath the trees.

By the morning of July 21 the rain had stopped, but the ground had turned into mud and we were still soaked to the skin. We got to our feet and looked about us to see whether the coast was clear. We wanted to go to a farmstead to get dry and clean up, but that was impossible, because the Germans were everywhere. We therefore moved to another field where we found some ditches. There, we dug in and prepared for the eventuality that the Germans might turn away from the woods and attack us. I ordered our men to spread out and be sure to move with great care so as not to set the corn stalks moving, for that would have given us away at once. Suddenly, I heard the sound of whistles. I was sure that the Germans had caught sight of us. I raised my head for a cautious look and to my relief saw the troops moving off abruptly toward the villages behind us. Soon, they had all vanished from view.

I heard a rumbling noise, as if a train was passing somewhere close by, and I wondered whether I had made a mistake reading the tattered map I still had with me from the Lublin days. The railroad line was supposed to be far away from where we had spent the night, certainly not close enough for us to hear the train so clearly. But somehow the quality of the sound was odd; it was not the sharp cadence of train wheels passing over railroad tracks. I turned to the man lying beside me and was about to ask his opinion. But before I could open my mouth to speak, the answer to my question came roaring past. Hiding out in the sopping fields that rainy July morning, we saw a strange parade, passing no more than fifty paces to our right; a seemingly unending line of tanks and military vehicles, followed by motorcycles bouncing along like so many rabbits on the run. This was, as we later learned, Hitler's much-vaunted army in retreat from the Russians. We lay flat on the ground, our faces down, afraid to make the slightest motion that might give us all away.

The sun had broken through the clouds. It was going to be a hot day. We lay in the field for what felt like hours, not daring to do as much as lift our heads as the pride of Germany's armed might thundered by, so close that, as we lay with our faces pressed to the ground, we had the illusion at times that the tanks, the trucks and the motorcycles were turning off into our field, to flatten us beneath their wheels like so many stalks of corn.

After what appeared endless hours, the noise gradually grew fainter, and finally ceased altogether. I raised my head. But now, from a great distance, there came a new sound, the low roar of explosions, one after the other. We did not know it then, but this was the sound of German army engineers blowing up their stalled tanks to make sure they would not be of any use to the Russians. I remained still, my face in the muddy soil.

At last the explosions, too, ceased. Cautiously, I lifted my head, then slowly rose to my knees. The sun, which I had last seen rising on the morning horizon, was now on the wane. We had spent a whole night and the better part of the following day lying on our bellies in the wet corn field, hiding from the Germans. I nudged the man beside me, and he passed the message along to the others. As far as I was able to tell, the coast was clear, at least for the time being. It took a while until we all were able to stand erect again. Then, we stumbled through the field, into the woods. There, under cover of the trees, we sank to the ground, utterly spent, soaked in sweat, our clothes stiff with caked mud. It was evening before we felt we could trust our cramped bodies to make it to the nearest village. Now that the immediate danger had passed, we needed food above all else. We came to a farmstead, where we got some bread and milk. Afterwards, we sat down in the grass just outside the village to decide where we should go next.

Suddenly, our lookout man pointed in the direction of the village. Someone was moving toward us. Like some portent, an old Polish peasant with flashing eyes and a flowing white beard, emerged out of the stalks of waving corn and pointed his walking stick straight at us like Moses' staff.

"What are you sitting here for? Get a move on. The Russians are already in Zeliszcze. You're free! Free, do you hear?"

The war was over!

*The author being honored at a testimonial dinner given on November
20, 1977 at the Americana Hotel in New York City. Left to right:
Jack Pomeranc, Joe Holm (Cholomski), Isaac Mendelson, Franek
Blaichman, Joseph Rolnick. Also seen in the lower right-hand corner
is Mrs. Samuel (Judith) Gruber.*

Epilogue

".... You're free. Free, do you hear?"

The words of the old peasant rang out prophetically in our ears. We were stupefied. Only slowly could we begin to realize what it meant. When the impact of what we had heard finally began to reach us, we leaped into the air shouting, laughing, dancing as if we had gone out of our minds, and then we raced toward Zeliszcze. As we came within sight of the first houses of the village, we remembered that we were soldiers, so we formed a straight line and marched, military fashion, as befitted members of a supposedly well-trained fighting force. But we were not prepared for the welcome we got there. The Russians opened fire on us. They later explained that they had taken us for Germans. It never occurred to them that mere partisan fighters could march in such a disciplined formation as we did. We dropped to the ground.

Then one of our men, Yurek Pomeranc, produced a white rag from his pants pocket, and frantically waved it as a sign of surrender. The shooting stopped and three of us walked toward the Russians. When they finally understood that we were not Nazis but Polish partisans, they gave us permission to proceed into the village and escorted us to their headquarters. Chil, another man

153

and I were invited into the tent where there were several high-ranking Russian officers, one of them a general. It turned out that a number of the officers were Jewish. They greeted us with open arms and plied us with questions as to where had we come from and whether we knew what had become of our families.

The Russian general told us that we could have as much food as we wanted; his men would be happy to share their rations. But he did not know what else he would be able to do for us. "As of tomorrow morning, you're on your own again," he said. "We still have a war on our hands, you know. There's an SS nest we have to clean out."

When we got back to Russian-occupied Lublin, we saw signs of the fierce fighting that had taken place only days before — burned-out tanks, dead horses, and human bodies decomposing in the hot sun. The city itself had not been badly damaged, but the streets were littered with corpses in German, Russian, and Polish uniforms.

The name of the Russian general in command of the occupied city was Nikita Khrushchev. The city was occupied by the Russian and regular Polish armies which had entered the city. When a parade was scheduled to celebrate liberation, we decided that all Jews who had participated in the struggle, either as partisans or as regular soldiers, should march together as a single unit to demonstrate that Jews also had helped in the active fight against Nazism. It was a moving moment when I accompanied a few Polish officers to the City Hall, where I helped to hoist the Polish flag.

Shortly afterwards, I had a sharp interchange with some of my Polish allies which set me thinking. General Withold had paid the Jewish partisans a visit and asked what we planned to do now that the fighting was over. Franek, the Polish partisan from Przypisowska who had helped us deal with troublesome elements from the "A.K.," interrupted my reply.

"What do you want?" he asked me harshly. "That they should paint a life-size portrait of you and hang it on the wall of head-quarters because you and your men were such heroes? Times have changed.

"The fighting is over. Poland has to be rebuilt. The days of adventures and rough-riding are past. There's real work for you to do now."

154

The question was, of course, whether I really wanted to make Poland my home after what I had experienced as a Jew in the war.

My first concern was with restoring what was left of Jewish life in Lublin, and I became one of the founders of the city's Jewish Council which had acquired two empty buildings, one to house refugees, and the other as a children's home which was called after the famous Jewish writer, J.L. Peretz. Hundreds of children who had survived the war hidden in the woods or with Polish farmers had drifted into Lublin, and I felt that it was up to the Jewish community to take the place of their parents.

As the capital of the new Polish Republic (Warsaw was not liberated until the following year) Lublin became a gathering place for thousands of survivors who had hidden in forests, bunkers, ghettos, and farmhouses, or had come from the death camps themselves. All these people had flocked to the city hoping to find surviving relatives and friends. Many had reason to believe that their relatives had fled into the Russian sector of Poland, east of the River Bug. Since communications between that sector and the area which the Russians had now liberated were non-existent, I put together a deputation to call on General Khrushchev to ask him for a permit so that these people could cross the river and try to learn the whereabouts of their families. Khrushchev kept us waiting for some time at Russian headquarters. Finally, he emerged from his office and brusquely demanded what we wanted. When he learned the purpose of our visit, he flatly replied, through an interpreter: *"Nyet.* Nobody will cross that border from here. If your relations are alive, they'll come to you." With that, he turned on his heel and left us.

I discovered that thousands of the Jews of Podhajce, my home town, had either been deported or gunned down on the spot and buried in mass graves that they themselves had been forced to dig. As for my own family, my father, mother, and two sisters had been shot by the Germans in June, 1943. My brother had been killed in a labor camp near Tarnopol. Only much later did I learn that some cousins, who had fled east into Russia and joined the Russian army, had survived.

During the first weeks following liberation, the Poles in Lublin were friendly to the Jews who flocked into the city. Some even invited them to parties arranged especially in their honor. But, when the newly formed Polish government, which had its seat in Lublin, decreed that Jewish survivors were entitled to reclaim their property which had been confiscated by the Germans, this stirred resentment among in Poles, many of whom had profited from what the Jews had lost and were now loath to give up their gains. Some Poles even seemed to think that too many Jews had managed to survive the gas chambers, and there were outbreaks of violence. When a man I knew from Markuszow tried to claim his home, which had passed into the possession of a Pole, the latter started an argument which ended with the Jew being killed.

When my working day was over, I could not bear to be alone in my lodgings. I spent all my free time with old friends and fellow partisans who had turned up in Lublin. One day in September, 1944, I visited Blimka Rubinstein who shared a two-room flat with a young girl who was introduced to me as Kristina Wietrzak. Blimka quickly explained that their friend's real name was Judith Jeleniewicz, that she had lived through the war as a Christian, and that her entire family had been killed by the Germans.

Judith and I were immediately attracted to each other. She was only 18 while I was past 30, but we shared the bleak sense of orphanhood that comes to all those, no matter what their age, who survive a deluge only to find themselves all alone in the world. I was not sure whether we should get married when everything was still so uncertain, but Judith believed in the future more than I did and insisted that she wanted a home of her own, and a new family. We were married on December 1, 1944. Ours was the first Jewish wedding to be held in Lublin since the liberation. Most of the guests were partisans and the ceremony was conducted by a Jewish chaplain from the Polish army. Judith had a dress made for her by one of her friends. The price was one large bag of flour!

Both Judith and I felt we could not raise a family in Poland after what we had experienced. Since the British had closed off Palestine, we decided to try to get to the United States. We left Europe in slow stages. From Lublin we moved westwards to Breslau, and from there to Prague in Czechoslovakia, where we received rations from the American Jewish Joint Distribution Committee. From there we went to Germany. When we arrived there, we had to stay in a displaced persons' camp organized by the Americans, while waiting for our turn to get to the United States. Meanwhile I became the administrator of a children's home in

Samuel Gruber and his wife, Judith (1945).

Prien, this organized by the Joint Distribution Committee. To this day I get letters from all over the United States, from Israel, and even from Australia, in which I learn about the progress of my "children." Usually they begin: "Dear Father ..."

Finally, in April, 1949, my American papers came through, and we left Europe bound for the United States. Making a living and adjusting to the conditions of a new country was not easy, but after my years with the partisans these challenges were comparatively simple. Yet it will be understandable that I should feel a special bond with others who, like myself, have shared some of my experiences in wartime Europe, particularly with the partisans.

157

It was really the crossing from Europe to America that marked the end of a whole phase in my life. For those born and raised in a free country it is very difficult to appreciate what I, and others like me, have gone through. It is for this reason that we feel it is so important to write accounts of the things that my friends and I have seen—the suffering and the heroism, our anguish and the eventual triumph of our fight against evil.

Samuel Gruber (1945).